Delights of Goa

Alda Figueiredo

Goa 1556   BROADWAY PUBLISHING HOUSE

Delights of Goa
© Alda Figueiredo alda_juliana@yahoo.co.uk

Co-published by

Goa,1556, Sonarbhat, Saligão 403511 Goa, India.
http://goa1556.goa-india.org, goa1556@gmail.com +91-832-2409490 and

BROADWAY
PUBLISHING HOUSE

Broadway Publishing House, a division of Goa's largest bookshop at Ashirwad,
18th June Rd, Panjim 403001 Ph/fax 6647038. http://broadwaybooksgoa.com

Cover design by Bina Nayak http://www.binanayak.com
Cover photos by Edgar Silveira and Frederick Noronha
Inside page layout by ManuGrafix
Printed and bound in India by Rama Harmalkar, 9326102225

Maps at the beginning of the book are courtesy Wikipedia.

ISBN 978-93-80739-21-2 Price: Rs. 195 in India.

Foreword

This is the first edition to the cookery book *The Goanese Fusion Flavours* published only in the United Kingdom in August 2005. This edition *Delight of Goa* includes thirty extra recipes and additional information on the history of Goa.

The recipes in this book have been adapted for Eastern and Western kitchens. The majority of the recipes are based on authentic Goan dishes. I have however also included recipes from two other continents, Africa and Europe; the reason being that my family and I have lived in these continents for over forty years and have developed the culinary taste of wonderful vegetable, meat and seafood dishes that characterises the international cuisine found in these continents.

It has given me great delight to bring together a range of wholesome and delicious food. Some of the recipes are simple and quick to make, others more elaborate, requiring a great many ingredients to achieve the mouth-watering and exotic taste of different foods. This book also gives an excellent description of the history, culture and produce of Goa. I hope you enjoy trying some of the recipes and are encouraged to visit this beautiful place.

Alda Figueiredo alda_juliana@yahoo.co.uk
March 2011

Acknowledgements

My thanks to my husband, sons, daughter, in-laws, grand-children, family and friends, who have tasted many of the recipes from this book, for their encouragement and constructive criticism. This has helped me to go forward and revise the recipes in order to improve the taste whenever necessary.

I also thank my friends and family who have shared their invaluable experience and contributed recipes for this book. I wish to express my appreciation to my niece Imelda and my friend Belinda, who jointly helped me to provide some of the Konkani words for the food glossary section.

I would like to acknowledge my debt and gratitude to Ian Collyer, ex-teacher of my children, for all his help and time given freely to examine its accuracy, style and proof-reading. I wish to thank my sons Max and Norman for their help and support with computer technology, photography and other ways.

Publishing history

First published in August 2005 in the United Kingdom as *The Goanese Fusion Flavours Cookery Manual* ISBN 978-0-9519019-3-9 © 2005 by Alda Figueiredo

British Library Cataloguing in Publication Data: A catalogue record for this book is available from the British Library.

First printed by Mail Boxes ETC. 113 High Street Ruislip, Middlesex HA4 8JN United Kingdom.

Reprinted in 2007 by: The Goa Archdiocesan Press NAP, Verna-Goa, India 0832 2782413, 2782416.

This edition by Goa,1556 and Broadway Publishing House.

The rights of Alda Figueiredo to be identified as the author of this work have been asserted in accordance with the Copyright, Design and Patents Act 1988.

Introduction

Goans have been living abroad for several generations, but the Goan identity is rooted, among other things, in a deep appreciation of food and drink.

My husband and I have been living abroad for over forty years, but our love for Goa is warm and we have been visiting Goa regularly over the years. Since our retirement we have been spending quality time in Goa every year. I have been cooking Goan food all my life, though I try dishes of other nationalities, such as English, Portuguese, Oriental and Italian and the cuisine from other parts of India. My children too have acquired a fondness for particular Goan dishes.

This book gives an update of Goan culture, history, produce and ingredients. The recipes bring out the fullest flavour of ingredients, whether it's by cooking curries, frying, oven-roasting or grilling.

Each year, over a couple of million tourists travel to Goa to enjoy the peace, good climate, golden beaches, warm hospitality and the exotic tastes of Goa. Goans are gregarious company, the very word *sussegad* literally implies living and enjoying life to the full. Though Goa became a part of India in 1961, evidence of 450 years of Portuguese rule is still apparent in the people's dress, language, religion and cuisine. Their particular appreciation for art, music and food sum up the images of Goan culture.

The basic components of Goan cooking are from local produce.

Coconut is the most important product used in cooking. Every part of the coconut is used for something: coconut oil, milk, and grated coconut flesh flavour many dishes. Desiccated coconut is one substitute for fresh coconut and can be used by adding it dry and straining it to create coconut milk. Nowadays a new product – coconut powder – is available in most countries. It is very finely ground dry coconut flesh, which has a creamier taste than desiccated and mixes well with water. The sap from the coconut palm, known as toddy, is also used to make vinegar and to act as a yeast substitute. The taste of Goa vinegar is very distinct and aromatic. It is ideal for preparing dishes, such as sorpatel, vindaloo and many of the preserves given in this book. I always take back to the UK a bottle or two from Goa for preparing my favourite delicacies. Another important product of the palm is jaggery, a dark coloured sweetener that is widely used in preparing Goan sweetmeats.

Rice is one of the most important food grains in the world and is the staple food of millions of people. Rice is supposed to have originated in India in about 5000 BCE. It is now produced in Asia, Africa, Latin America, parts of Europe, Australia and the United States. Asian countries grow a large amount of rice for their own consumption, whereas the United States is the largest exporters of rice. Most varieties of rice grow on land submerged in water; therefore it is cultivated just before the start of the monsoon period.

Goa and large parts of India are major rice producers and enthusiastic rice eaters. Rice and fish curry is the staple food of Goans. During the Portuguese reign, Goa was an agrarian economy with the focus on rice, the staple diet of the people of Goa. Goa's local paddy cultivation was extensive – four times greater than the area under cultivation of other crops, like coconut, fruits, cereals, legumes and vegetables. Every household would cultivate paddy fields owned by the people or the local communities in Goa. Sadly some of the fields are now converted into colonies of residential or commercial buildings.

Paddy fields make vivid splashes of intense green colour during the monsoon, which is splendid to look at. The way of living has changed in recent decades. Very few households cultivate paddy fields, because the labour cost is too expensive. Rice meals are a meal in themselves, although other variety of dishes is made of rice: such as *sanna*, rice *pori*, *coiloris* (rice bread), *arroz* and rice pudding.

Goan cooking generally involves liberal amount of spices, giving dishes a strong taste and distinctive aroma. The most commonly used ingredients are cumin, coriander, chillies, garlic, ginger, pepper, asafoetida and turmeric. Particular combinations of spices have led to a number of styles of cooking, which have different flavours – masala, vindaloo, *rechear*, xacuti, *assad* and balchao (rich, spicy tomato) being some of the most famous. The Portuguese cuisine is a great influence in Goan cooking.

After my retirement I have been visiting Goa every year for a couple of months or more and have visited quite a number of restaurants. However, I have noticed that the names of some of the Portuguese dishes have almost disappeared. Hence my desire to include in this book the recipes for dishes prepared by our ancestors, in addition to other international cuisine I frequently prepare for my family. The recipes are illustrated in some instances with photographs of the dishes.

History of Goa

Goa is a tiny state of India situated along the Western Ghats of the Deccan Plateau along the Konkan coast, which has a wider costal strip that includes the states of Goa and Kerala.

Goa is green and fertile and has rice fields, coconut trees and tropical fruit trees, namely, mango, caju, guavas, jackfruits and papayas. It covers 3,702 sq km and consists of two districts North and South Goa. The capital of Goa is Panaji (Panjim), situated at the mouth of the River Mandovi.

Goa was a former Portuguese colony and remained under Portuguese rule for 450 years. Goa was formerly known as *Goa Dourada* (Golden Goa), *Rainha de Oriente* (Queen of the East) and *Roma de Oriente* (Rome of the East). In early times Goa was the major port for its rich hinterland, and had a flourishing trade with sea-faring nations, such as Italy, Arabia, Eritrea and Ethopia. Arab traders had settled on the Konkan Coast centuries before Muslim conquests.

Goa is the smallest state of India, which certainly appear to be insignificant compared to size and magnitude of the rest of India. Somehow Goa has a distinctive atmosphere of its own and is a major national and international attraction. This tiny state of India remained cut off from the wider subcontinent by a wall of mountains, tidal rivers and the sea.

Before the Portuguese invaded Goa in 1510, the country was ruled by a succession of powerful Hindu dynasties, who installed puppet governors from their capitals in India.

In 420 CE, the Kadambas gradually came to dominate the region, forging marital alliance with their powerful neighbours. In 973 the Kadamba's old allies, the Chalukyas, defeated their rivals, the Rashtrakutas. At this point the Goan kings took this as their opportunity to oust the Governors from their capital Chandrapura (now known as Chandor), which they invaded by placing a fleet of ships side by side to form a bridge across the Zuari River.

The Kadambas ruled Goa for two and half centuries (1006 to 1356) until its conquest by Mahmud Gawan on behalf of his Bahamani master. In 1470 he brought Goa under the rule of Bahamani dynasty and Goa became the most important town of their kingdom.

Around this period two different empires emerged one after another. The rulers of Vijayanagar captured Goa. The Bahamani's efforts to expand their holdings led to frequent conflicts with the Vijayanagar Kingdom. During this period of great upheaval, the General of Mahmud Gawan, defeated Vijayanagar and recaptured Goa. As a consequence of continual fighting on the Deccan Plateau, Bijapur lost Goa to the Portuguese in 1510. In addition to their stronghold of Goa, the Portuguese established outposts at Daman and Diu along the Gujarat coast with the help of the Sultanate of Gujarat, who disliked the Arabs and had a fear of a Turco-Egyptian involvement.

The story of the opening of doors to foreign rule in India is an interesting one.

In 1497, Vasco da Gama reached the port of Calicut in search of spices. The most popular spice, black peppercorn, was discovered by him in the southern part of the west coast of India – the Malabar Coast – which is still famed for the quality of its pepper.

In the sixteenth century, the Portuguese established formidable trade power in Goa. In 1509 Alfonso Albuquerque began his masterly six years in command of the Portuguese interests in the east and felt that the conquest of Goa would strengthen the Portuguese rule over the Arabian Sea.

In March 1510, Alfonso Albuquerque sailed up the River Mandovi and captured Goa (the area subsequently known as Old Goa). It was a very short-lived success. Yusuf Adil Shah, the Governor of Bijapur, drove the Portuguese into the sea. In November 1510, the Portuguese returned with larger forces and recaptured Goa and ruled the region for over 450 years.

Finally, Goa saw the end of Portuguese rule on December 19, 1961 and is now the 25th state and part of the Republic of India. India was ruled by Europeans after the 16th century, namely Portuguese, French, Dutch and English. By the end of the 17th century, the Portuguese lost most of their territories to the Dutch and English only retaining Goa, Daman, Diu and a few enclaves.

Today, Goa is one of India's most popular holiday destinations with its idyllic beaches, which stretch 100km from north to south, lush paddy fields, coconut plantations, colourful villages, forts, Hindu temples and magnificence churches and cathedrals built around the 16th century by the Portuguese. Many of these have a special history and therefore deserve a special visit to appreciate its beauty. The palm fringed coast is interrupted at places by the sparkling estuaries of the Mandovi, Zuari, Sal and other small rivers.

Goans are an easy going people who often go out of their way to make visitors feel at home. Goa is an irresistible blend of the Indian and the Portuguese. The pace of life in Goa has picked up over the past thirty years. Economical, social and cultural changes have created more jobs for the local and brought in prosperity. Adversely, these factors have also created different types of problems.

Vegetables in Goa are plentiful, such as cabbage, long beans, bitter gourd, carrots, cauliflower, different types of spinach, white or ash gourd, kohlrabi, beetroot, potatoes, sweet potatoes, cucumber, okra, onions, peas, pepper, aubergine, turnip, radishes, pumpkin and marrow. Vegetarian meals can be as rich as non-vegetarian meals, because a great variety of vegetables and pulses can be found in Goa.

I have, therefore, included a separate section for vegetable dishes. Every meal should include a green vegetable, which can be a main dish or an accompaniment to the main dish. Green vegetables make an invaluable contribution towards the supply of minerals and vitamins. They are low in calories and high in fibre. They add essential qualities to the diet, which assist in digestion. Vegetable meals lack protein and to achieve this vital component it is prudent to add dried beans, grains and soya products to the diet when necessary.

Seafood

Goa is famous for its seafood, the classic dish being fish curry and rice. Local cooks can offer a mouth-watering choice with the variety and range on offer, such as kingfish, pomfret, shark, rock salmon, mullet, sardines, skate, mackerel, Bombay ducks and so many other varieties of river fish. Among the excellent shellfish available are crabs, prawns, tiger prawns, lobsters and crayfish. Other seafood includes squids, oysters, clams, cockles, whelks and mussels. My family's favourite dish is *ambot tik*, a slightly sour curry dish that can be prepared with either fish or meat, but more usually fish.

Meats

Sorpatel is the regional dish of Goa, and is prepared from pork, pork liver, heart and kidneys. These are diced and cooked in a thick and very spicy sauce flavoured with feni. Sorpatel, like *balchao*, keeps for several days, and is actually considered to taste better if left for three or four days before consumption. Xacuti is a Goan speciality. The recipe in this book is used by the chefs at one of the old top local hotels, established during the Portuguese rule. Xacuti has a traditional way of preparing meat, usually chicken or lamb, by cooking a variety of roasted spices and coconut milk to give a distinctive and delicious flavour. Pork and beef is widely used by Catholics. Pork Vindaloo is another Goan speciality. It is famous for its fiery heat and should be served with plain boiled rice to bring out its distinctive taste.

Chouricos are spicy pork sausages, which owe more than a passing debt to Portuguese culinary traditions. Goan sausages are prepared using well salted and spiced cubes of pork. Once they have been made, the strings of sausages are dried in the sun and then hung above the fire where they are gradually smoked. Traditionally they have been eaten during the monsoon, when fish is scarce.

Sweetmeats

The most famous of Goa's sweetmeats is *bebinca*, a wonderful concoction made with layer upon layer of coconut pancakes. Cooking the perfect bebinca is an art form, for not only does the cook have to get exactly the right mixture of egg yolk, flour, coconut milk and sugar, but the cooking has to be timed just right to ensure that all layers are cooked equally. Dodol is another famous Goan sweet, traditionally eaten at Christmas time, and made with rice flour, coconut milk, jaggery, sugar and cashew nuts. *Doce De Grão* (gram sweet with coconut) is a well-loved festive sweet, prepared during Christmas and other important family occasions or festivals.

Fruits

Quite a few varieties of fruits are available in Goa, such as banana, coconut, guava, chikoo, cashew nuts, different varieties of mangoes, melon, pineapple, plum, pomegranate, *boram*, *santra*, cajus, jackfruit and *sitaford*. Some of the tropical fruits are only available during the hot summer season from March to May. Most Goans working in other parts of India have traditionally visit Goa during this period.

Alcholic drinks

The most famous Goa's tipple is 'feni'. There are two types of feni, both of which are made from local ingredients. Coconut or palm feni is made from the sap drawn from the severed shoots from a coconut tree. In Goa it is known as toddy, and the men who collect it are called toddy tappers.

Toddy tappers at work are a common sight, though fewer now than in the past. They crouch in the canopy of the palm tree to collect the pot that has filled with creamy white sap, then trim the shoots to facilitate further collection, tie a new pot over the top and descend to move on to the next tree.

Caju (cashew) feni can only be made during the cashew season in late March and early April. Cashews are an important crop in Goa. From early spring you can see the cashew trees in full bloom.

The cashew apple, when ripe, turns into a yellow-orange colour and the nut ripens below it. When the fruit is harvested, the nuts are separated from the 'apples' and are laid out to dry in the sun. When the nuts are dried, they are roasted and then shelled by hand. The apples, meanwhile, are placed in a pit and trampled by foot to collect the juice.

Both palm toddy and juice can be drunk fresh immediately after collection and are reputed to be delicious. Left for just a few hours, however, they soon start to ferment.

Caju is also used as a raising agent in breads and cakes. The caju distillation is a complex and arduous task. The alcoholic strength of caju feni is around 30% or 35%, comparable to whisky. The milder concoction is known as *urac*. It is delicious with sugar and Limca. Both coconut and caju liqueur are used as an aperitif and also used as a preservative in pork dishes.

Contents

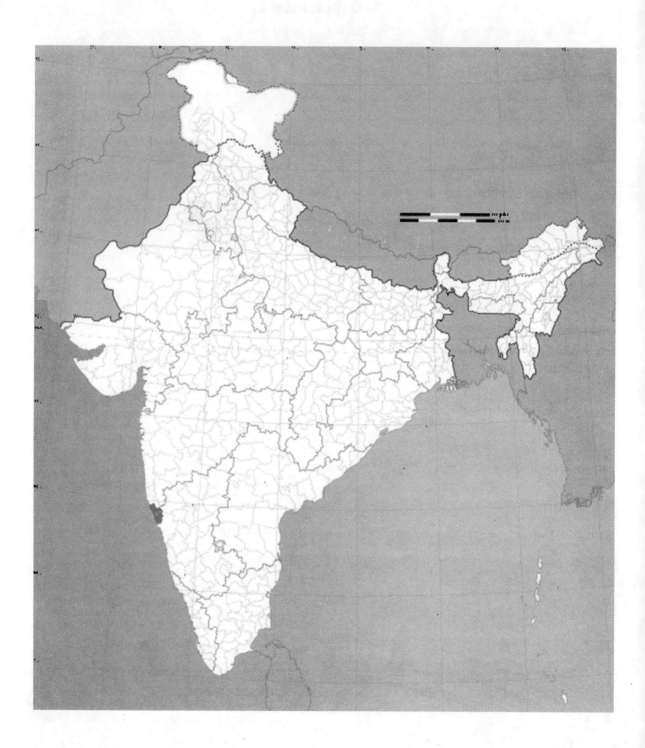

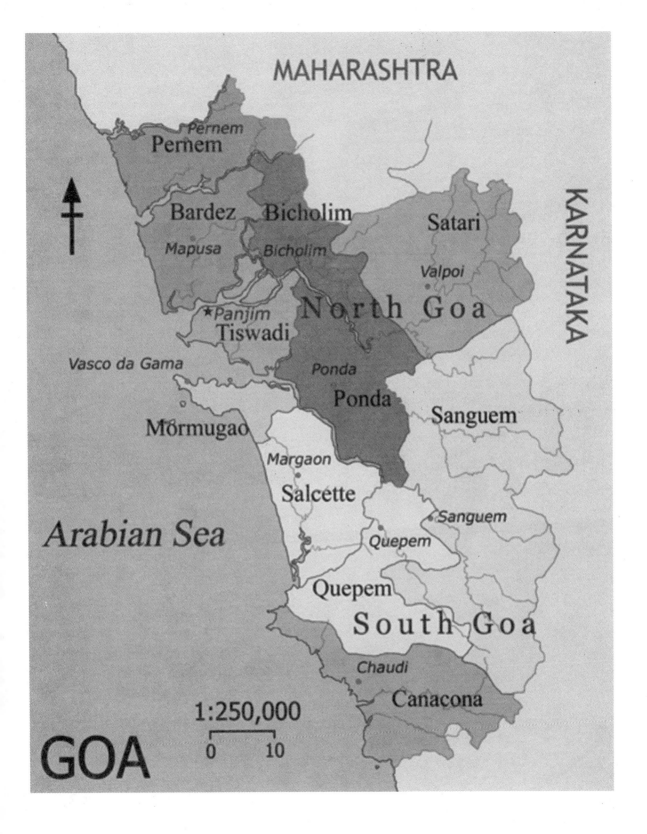

Herbs from my garden

Parsley

Sage

Thyme

Coriander

Madras Curry leaves

Oregano

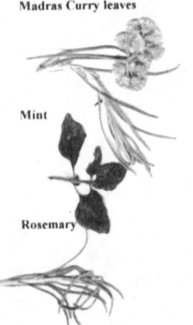

Mint

Tea Mint

Rosemary

French Terragon

Chives

Sweet Basil

Commonly used Goan Ingredients

Kashmiri chillies: The most popular chillies are Kashmiri chillies.

Their flavour is mild, but the fiery red colour gives distinctive taste to the dish. Goa has a variety of locally grown chillies and one's preference depends on each individual taste for pungency.

Goa jaggery: Made up of palm extract and is dark brown in colour. It is used in coconut-based sweets.

Bimbli: Sour, gherkin-shaped fruit, used as a souring agent. It can be used for chutney and pickle.

Bitter Gourd: It is from the marrow family, a dark green-skinned vegetable and has a bitter taste. To decrease its bitterness it should be soaked in salt water. Their bitter taste should not be eliminated completely, as it is prized for cleansing the blood. Before cooking the outer skin is slightly scraped. The pulp and the large seeds embedded in it should be discarded.

Cocum: A deep red grape-sized berry. The skin when dried is black in colour and used as a souring agent for fish and vegetable dishes.

Mango solam: Raw mango, peeled, sliced, preserved in salt and dried in the sun until it turns very firm and solid. It is a souring agent in fish and certain vegetables.

Tiporam/Tefla: Dried, acrid, lemon-flavoured berries. Mostly used in curries with mackerel and other fish with a high fat content.

Bombil or Bombay duck is a slim, soft fish. It is delicious when fried with batter or breadcrumbs. When fresh fish is scarce in the monsoon season the dried bombil is the perfect accompaniment to fish curry and rice.

Dried prawns: are commonly used in coconut curries and vegetable dishes, relishes and chutneys.

Black pepper: There are two types of pepper white and black. They are used whole, freshly ground or as powder.

Bay leaves: Dried leaves of the bay laurel tree, used in flavouring many foods.

Cardamon (ilchi): is an important curry spice, strong and aromatic. The pod contains small seeds which are crushed into powder.

Cinnamon: (tikki) it is the bark of the tree and used whole cinnamon stick or powder form. It is used extensively in meat curries and in desserts and cakes. It has a sweet, warm and aromatic taste.

Cloves: (Kalafuram) An important curry spice, pungent and aromatic. It can be used whole or powdered form.

Coriander (dhania): used extensively in seed and powder form. It has a gentle and fragrant spice which balances the hotter spices in curries. Coriander leaves are used to garnish most of the Indian dishes. It can be used as an ingredient in salad, chutneys and curries.

Cumin (jeera): It has a warm and aromatic taste. It is also available in powder form. It is good for the digestive system and very popular in curries.

Fenugreek seeds: (Methi) Used whole or ground in curries. It has a strong aroma and bitter taste. It is used extensively in pickles and some vegetable dishes. Fenugreek leaves are used as a vegetable dish.

Garlic (Losun): A white pungent bulb which separates into cloves. It is used extensively in Indian curries to add flavour to all types of food. It has a strong smell when cooked and is also used as a medicinal component.

Ginger (alem): It comes from the root of a tropical plant. Available in powdered form, preserved in sugar or used fresh. The amount to be used depends according to one's taste.

Lemon grass: can be grown in the garden or bought in dried form.

Lime Juice: Lime is a member of the citrus family. Similar to lemon juice and can be used as a substitute for vinegar.

Mint: used in salad, chutneys, as a curry ingredient and as a garnish. Dried mint is available, but not very effective.

Mustard seeds: (rai) tiny round blackish- reddish-brown seeds which are used throughout India for pickling and for seasoning. They are used whole or crushed in curries. They have a strong, hot flavour and are used in small quantities.

Nutmeg: It is a musk-scented nut. It is hard aromatic seed which can be grated into fine powder to use in Goan sweets and curries.

Onion (piau or Kandhe): It is used extensively as the base for most curries– it is sliced or chopped then fried golden brown. When fried it caramelises the sugar and releases the delicious flavour and aroma. Red and white onions are used in salads.

Pappadums: Paper- thin lentil cakes, which may be bought in packets at supermarkets and speciality stores. When fried in hot oil they swell, curl and double in size.

Semolina (sujee): Grain made from wheat, commonly used to make puddings and sweets.

Saffron: It is a very expensive spice. To bring out the flavour and colour of saffron to its fullest, it is best to dry-roast it first. Put the required amount in a small, heavy frying pan over a low flame. Stir it until the threads turn a very dark reddish-brown colour or crumble the threads into a small amount of hot milk. Let the saffron soak for a few hours and then use this milk to tint and flavour rice or whatever else you want.

Sesame seeds: Extremely nutty and flavoursome. They are a high source of protein and calcium. Sesame seeds are used throughout Asia in dishes from main course to salads and desserts. A fragrant oil made out of these seeds is used in Chinese dishes or can be stir-fried in small quantities to enrich the taste of the dish.

Tamarind pulp: (Ambli) It is a common Goan curry ingredient. The pod of the tamarind tree is dried in the sun – the outer shell and the seeds are removed and preserved by applying a little salt. It is rich in vitamin – it gets its name from the Arabic 'tamar-I-hind or 'the dates from India'. Goa produces a very large quantity of tamarind pulp. The tree is massive in size depending on its age. To make tamarind juice, soak a piece of tamarind (a size of a plum) in ½ cup of hot water and allow to stand for 10 minutes. Squeeze the tamarind pulp to extract the juice – discard the pulp. It is a substitute for lime or lemon juice or vinegar.

Tamarind paste: This substance is concentrated and comes in a jar. It is a convenient method of adding tamarind paste to curry. One tablespoon of tamarind is equivalent to 1½ tablespoons of lime or 3 tablespoons of vinegar.

Turmeric (Haldi): A golden-yellow fragrant spice used extensively to give colour and flavour to curries, vegetables, rice and savouries.

Yoghurt (Dahi) Milk curds – it can be used to enrich salads, as a curry ingredient or as a curry accompaniment to reduce the pungency.

Commonly used spices in Goan food

Red Chilly	Black pepper	Cumin
Cloves	Cinnamon	Cardoman
Coriander	Fenugreek	Garlic
Ginger	Mustard	Nutmeg
Saffron	Sesame	Turmeric

Weights & Measures

The recipes in this book are given in both metric and American measures. As it is difficult to give an exact conversion, the nearest equivalent is shown in the tables below. All spoon measurements used throughout this book are level unless specified otherwise. In Indian and Goan cooking a few extra grams of some of the ingredients, such as onions or tomatoes or ginger, will not make much of a difference. Similarly a few extra millilitres of water will not make any difference. So rest easy when you use the measures given for these recipes!

Abbreviations

tsp	teaspoon	**fl oz**	fluid ounce
oz	ounce	**pt**	pint
tbsp	tablespoon	**lb**	pound
g	gram	**qt**	quart
kg	kilogram	**l**	litre
dtsp	dessert tablespoon		

Conversion of grams into ounces

1	gram	=	0.035	ounces
10	grams	=	0.35	ounces
100	grams	=	3.5	ounces
200	grams	=	7.0	ounces
300	grams	=	10.5	ounces
400	grams	=	14	ounces
500	grams	=	1 lb 1.5	ounces
600	grams	=	1 lb 5	ounces
700	grams	=	1 lb 8	ounces
800	grams	=	1 lb 12	ounces
900	grams	=	2 lb	
1000	grams	=	2 lb 3.5	ounces

The following table gives the approximate measures of metric and imperial units :-

Ounces	Nearest Equivalent
1	28 gm
2	57gm
3	85gm
4	113gm
5	142gm
6	170gm
7	198gm
8	227gm
9	255gm
10	284gm
11	312gm
12	340gm
13	369gm
14	397gm
15	425gm
16 or 1 lb	454gm
1 lb 8 ounces	700gm
2 lb	900gm
3 lb 3oz	1.5 kg

The following chart converts from American measures to metric measures :-

American Measures	Metric
1 teaspoon (tsp)	5 g
2 tsp	10g
3 tsp	15g
6 tsp	30g or 2 Tbsp
1 Tbsp (tablespoon)	15g
1 Tbsp	3tsp or ½ oz
¼ cup	4 Tbsp or 2 oz
½ cup	5 Tbsp +2 tsp
2/3 cup	10 Tbsp +2 tsp
1 cup	16 Tbsp or 8 oz
¾ cup	12 Tbsp or 6 oz
1 cup (liquid measure)	237ml
1 oz (dry measure)	28g
16 fl oz (liquid measure)	2 cups or 1 pint
2 pints (liquid measure)	4 cups or 1 quart
8fl oz (liquid measure)	1 cup or ½ pt
4 fl oz (liquid measure)	½ cup or ¼ pt
1 pt (liquid measure)	2 cups or ½ quart

The following table gives the approximate measures of metric and imperial units.

Ounces (fl oz)	Pints (pt)	Millilitres (ml)
3.5 oz	1/6 pt	100
5 oz	¼ pt	150
10 oz	½ (pt)	300
15 oz	¾ (pt)	420
20 oz	1 (pt)	560
25 oz	1 ¼ (pt	700
30 oz	1 ½ (pt)	850
35 oz	1 ¾ (pt|)	1000
40 oz	2 (pt)	1120

The following chart will give a convenient guide to convert the commonly used ingredients in this book:-

Rice	1 cup	200g
All dals (lentils)	1 cup	200g
All dry beans	1 cup	200g
Semolina	1 cup	200g
Wheat flour	1 cup	120g
Cornflour	1 cup	80g
Breadcrumbs	1 cup	100g
Castor sugar	1 cup	120g
Raisins	1 cup	145g
Clarified butter	1 cup	260g
Granulate sugar	1 cup	120g
Ghee or Margarine	1 cup	200g
Coconut (grated)	1 cup	80g
Coconut (desiccated)	1 cup	60g
Coconut paste	1 cup	260g

Various Spices

Peppercorns	1 tsp	3.3g
Peppercorns	1 tbsp	10g
Coriander seeds	1 tsp	2g
Coriander seeds	1 tbsp	6g
Cumin seeds	1 tsp	3g
Cumin seeds	1 tbsp	9g
Fennel seeds	1 tsp	2.5g
Fenugreek seeds	1 tbsp	7.5g
All powdered spices	1 tsp	5g

Liquids

Lemon juice	1 cup	240ml
Water	1 cup	240ml
Cream	1 cup	240ml
Groundnut oil	1 cup	200ml
Mustard oil	1 cup	220ml
Milk	1 cup	240ml

Oven Temperatures

Gas Mark 1	275 F	140 C
Gas Mark 2	300 F	150 C
Gas Mark 3	325 F	170 C
Gas Mark 4	350 F	180 C
Gas Mark 5	375 F	190 C
Gas Mark 6	400 F	200 C
Gas Mark 7	425 F	220 C
Gas Mark 8	450 F	230 C
Gas Mark 9	475 F	240 C

SPICE POWDERS

Spice Powders

Five different spice mixtures are used consistently in this recipe book. The ingredients are given in metric and American measures. Using whole spices is more effective when preparing these mixtures than using ready-made spice powders. These mixtures can be stored in airtight jars for up to six months.

Spice No.1 (Sambar masala) is used for vegetables, pulses, dried fish curry and meat dishes.

Ingredients

15 dry red chillies
1 tsp cumin seeds
2 tbsp coriander seeds
½ tsp fenugreek seeds
½ tsp asafoetida
4 curry leaves
3 tbsp desiccated coconut
1 tsp oil

Fry in oil the chillies, curry leaves, coriander seeds and asafoetida for a minute, then add the coconut and cumin seeds and fry for another minute. Lastly add the fenugreek seeds and fry till the coconut turns light brown. Cool the ingredients then put them in a blender and blend into a smooth dry powder. Add 1 teaspoon of turmeric powder and mix well. Store it in an airtight jar.

Spice No. 2 is used for meat and vegetable dishes (Jeerem Mirem and caldin dishes)

Ingredients

18g / 3 tablespoons coriander seeds
18g / 2 tablespoons cumin seeds
10g / 1 tablespoon black pepper
40 cloves
20 pods cardamoms
2 x 3 inch cinnamon pieces

Grind the above ingredients in a blender into a smooth powder. Add 1 teaspoon of turmeric powder and store in an airtight jar.

Spice No. 3 is used for fish, poultry and vegetable dishes

Ingredients

15g /1 ½ teaspoon red chilli powder
65g / 4½ tablespoon of cumin seed powder
30g / 3 teaspoon black powder
15g / 1½ teaspoon turmeric powder

Mix all the above ingredients together and store in an airtight jar.

Spice Mixture No. 4 is also known as Garam Masala

Ingredients

45g / 3 tablespoon of black pepper
20g / 2" of cloves
2 x 3" cinnamon pieces
15 pods of cardamom
60g / 4 tbsp coriander seeds
2.5g / 1 tsp fenugreek
2.5g / 1 tbsp mace
9 g / 1 tbsp cumin
5 dried bay leaves

Grind the above ingredients into dry powder and add 1 teaspoon of nutmeg powder. Mix thoroughly and store in an airtight jar.

Spice No. 5 is used for fish and meat preparations

Ingredients

100 g or 3.5 ounces of Kashmiri chillies
9 g / 1 tablespoon cumin seeds
25 black peppercorns
12 cloves
2 inch cinnamon stick
12 cloves of garlic
2 x 1 inch ginger
2.2g / ½ teaspoon turmeric powder
2 teaspoons tamarind
¼ teaspoon of salt
½ teaspoon of sugar

Grind the chillies and all the above spices in vinegar and store in an airtight and sterilised jar. Do not use water.

Tandoori Masala Powder

Tandoori dishes are very popular nowadays. It is a good idea to make up a batch of tandoori masala for use as and when required.

4 tablespoons of paprika powder
4   "   of ground coriander
4   "   of ground cumin
3 tablespoons of ground ginger
Food colouring is optional

Method

Mix the above spices thoroughly in a bowl then keep in a sterile jar, out of sunlight.

PASTE AND MASALA

Paste and Masala

It is a convenient process to prepare in advance some of the ingredients we use for daily cooking such as garlic, ginger, coriander paste and various other masalas. These can also be purchased in many British supermarkets.

Garlic Paste

Ingredients

200 gm of garlic peeled and cut roughly
1 teaspoon of peppercorns
½ teaspoon of salt
1 tablespoon lemon juice or vinegar
1 tbsp olive oil
6 green chillies cut roughly

Method

Grind or put all the ingredients in the blender and blend into a fine paste. Do not use water. Store it in an airtight jar. Use as desired. It can be kept in the fridge for up to three months.

Green Chilli and Coriander Paste

This paste is delicious with beef or chicken dishes. Apply two tablespoons to the meat and marinate for about one hour, giving the meat one good stir after half an hour. Or add a teaspoon for any meat curry to give extra flavour. It can be kept in the refrigerator for up to six weeks. It can also be used to stuff fish, instead of rechear masala.

Ingredients

1 tablespoon of olive oil
15 green chillies chopped
2 bunches of fresh coriander washed and chopped
½ teaspoon of salt
2 tablespoon lemon juice or vinegar
1½ tsp sugar

Method

To make the paste, put all the above ingredients into a food processor or blender then switch on to a high speed and blend until you have a smooth-looking paste. Remove the paste and put it in the sterilised bottle. Always ensure that the bottle is well sealed every time you use it. You can also grind the ingredients with a grinding stone – the results are often much better.

Garlic and Ginger Paste

Ingredients

200 gms of garlic, peeled and cut roughly
75 gms of ginger peeled and chopped roughly
2 green chillies chopped
½ tsp of salt
1 tablespoon of vinegar

Method

Put all the ingredients in the blender and blend into a fine paste. Do not use water. Store it in an airtight and sterilised jar. It is a very useful paste for any meat dish and saves a lot of time. It can remain in the fridge for up to three months.

Tandoori Paste

Ingredients

600 ml (1 pt) plain yoghurt
1 small onion coarsely chopped
2 garlic cloves chopped
1 inch piece of fresh root ginger
2 green chillies roughly sliced
3 tsp garam masala

Method

1. Combine the yoghurt, onion, garlic, ginger, chillies and garam masala in a blender or food processor and blend until smooth.

2. Strain the paste through a coarse sieve into a large bowl, pushing through as much liquid as possible.

Red Curry Paste

Ingredients

115g/4oz dark red onions or shallots, sliced
10 red chillies, seeded and sliced or 1 ½ tsp chilli powder
1 tbsp of vine vinegar
3 lemon grass stalks, lower part of stem sliced and bruised
1 ½ ginger, peeled, sliced and the stems from the coriander sprigs,(stems only)
2 tbsp ground oil
1 tsp grated rind of green lime
1 ½ tsp of coriander seeds
1 tsp cumin seeds
1 tsp salt
1 tbsp dried prawns

Method

1. Place in the grinder the chillies, onions, garlic, lemon grass, ginger, dried prawns, vinegar and the stems from the coriander sprigs and grind to a smooth paste, gradually adding the oil. Add the grated rind of lemon.

2. Roast the coriander and cumin seeds, then turn them into a clean mortar and grind them to a powder. Add the ground spices to the paste with salt and mix well.

3. The same ingredients can be used to make the green curry paste. In place of red chillies use green chillies and white onion instead of red onions and leaves of coriander to enhance the colour.

Chilli Sauce

Ingredients

2 fresh red chilli seeded and finely chopped
1 teaspoon ground garlic or very finely chopped
1 dessert spoon fish sauce or soy sauce
1 dessert spoon lime juice
1 dessert spoon white vinegar
3 dessertspoon water
2 tbsp sugar

Method

Mix well all the ingredients until the sugar is dissolved. Serve with spring rolls, wontons or paper wrapped fish.

This masala goes well with fish, fowl and white meat. Every Goan household keeps a supply handy. Nowadays this masala is available in most of the food stores, but does not taste as good as the home-made combination.

Ingredients

25 red Kashmiri chillies
1 teaspoon cumin seeds
10 cloves of garlic peeled
15 peppercorns
2 inches piece of ginger peeled
1 oz dried tamarind
1oz dried seedless plums
1 cup of vinegar
1 teaspoon of turmeric powder
1 teaspoon of sugar
Salt to taste

Method

1. Grind chillies and all the above spices, plums and tamarind together in vinegar to form a smooth paste. Do not use a drop of water. Alternatively, place all the ingredients into a food processor and blend until you have a smooth looking paste.

2. Add sugar, salt and turmeric powder. Mix well.

3. Put it in a tightly sealed bottle and it can be left in the refrigerator for up to six months or a year.

4. This masala can be used to prepare rechear masala of pomfret, mackerel, Kingfish and so on.

Hollandaise Sauce

Home made Hollandaise sauce is exceedingly delicious. I have watched Delia Smith preparing this recipe on her television series. It goes well with any filleted fish which has a lovely firm, meaty texture. Serve with boiled potatoes and fresh vegetables.

Ingredients

2 medium size eggs, separated
1 dessertspoon white wine vinegar
1 dessertspoon lemon juice
4oz (110g) salted butter
Salt and freshly milled black pepper

Method

1. Separate the eggs. Place the egg yolks in a food processor then add salt and freshly milled black pepper. Switch on and blend the ingredients thoroughly. Place the egg whites in a separate bowl.

2. In a small saucepan heat the vinegar and lemon juice till the mixture simmers.

3. Switch on the food processor again and pour the hot liquid on to the egg yolks in a steady stream.

4. In the same saucepan melt the butter gently; do not allow to brown. When the butter is turned into liquid and foaming, switch on the processor again and pour in the butter in a steady thin stream, until all the butter is incorporated and the sauce is thickened.

5. Whisk the egg whites until they form soft peaks. Fold the sauce, a tablespoon at a time, into the egg whites. Taste and see if seasoning is required.

6. The sauce is now ready to serve.

7. To re-heat the sauce, place the bowl over slightly simmering water to warm through gently.

Bechamel sauce is quite a useful sauce and can be used for quite a few recipes of fish and Italian dishes, ie. Moussaka and Lasagne. There are several variations to this recipe using different herbs. It is also available in packets. Instructions on preparing the sauce are given below.

Ingredients

3 tbsp butter
1 small onion finely cut
3 tbsp flour
1 pt milk
Small sprig of thyme & 1 bay leaf (optional)
Pinch of pepper and nutmeg

Method

1. Melt the butter in a heavy saucepan. Sauté the onion until transparent.

2. Remove the pan from the heat, stir in the flour, then cook gently over low heat for 3-5 minutes, stirring constantly until flour is well coated. Add a quarter of the milk, stirring vigorously.

3. Add herbs, pepper and nutmeg to taste.

4. When sauce begins to thicken, add the remaining half of the milk, stirring all the time until the sauce begins to thicken again. Now add all the remaining milk, stir constantly until sauce begins to bubble.

5. Simmer for at least 5 - 8 minutes, so that the ingredients are well blended and the sauce is thick and creamy without lumps.

STARTERS

Vegetable Samosa

The triangular mince-vegetable-filled patties look complicated to make, but it is well worth having a go. It takes a little practice to get a good shape, which does not burst when deep-fried. Once you've got the hang of it, you will be able to prepare them fairly easily. It is always better to practise with a small quantity. You will be surprised how easy it is to make this delicious hors d'oeuvre or snack. You can make them in advance and freeze them for up to three months.

Ingredients

For pastries:

Corn oil for deep frying and sealing
1lb (450g) strong white plain flour

For Vegetable filling:

1 teaspoon black pepper ground
2 teaspoon chilli powder
4 teaspoons salt
1 large carrot peeled and cut into
cubes not larger than peas
2 tablespoon fresh coriander
2 tablespoons corn oil

2 lb (900g) potatoes mashed
1 lb (450g) frozen peas
2 large onions finely cut
2 teaspoons ground coriander
1 teaspoon ground cumin
1 dessertspoon of dry fenugreek leaves

Method

1. Add approximately 4 dessertspoons of corn oil to the flour, and enough water to make dough. Knead well until the dough leaves the sides of the bowl clean. Leave it to stand for at least 1 hour.

2. Heat two tablespoon of oil and add onions and fry until soft then add carrots and frozen peas. Cover the pan and cook for about three minutes. Add mashed potatoes, salt, and spices, except fresh coriander. Mix all the ingredients well then add fresh coriander. Leave it to cool.

3. Make a flour and water paste (to glue samosas together) and put a little corn oil in a bowl (for brushing discs at stage 4)

4. Divide the rested dough into 10 balls and roll each ball about 1½ inches (4cm) in diameter then roll into discs of 4 inches (10 cm) in diameter. Brush each disc with corn oil on one side. Sprinkle with a little flour and join two together. Brush the top side of the second disc with oil and sprinkle with flour as the first then add the third disc. Continue placing five discs on top of each other by brushing each top disc with oil and sprinkle with flour. Make two similar batches of five discs. Roll the first batch of discs out to circles 8 inches (20 cm) in diameter. Heat a large enough pan on medium temperature and cook for about one minute. Turn and repeat (it should bubble slightly). Clean the frying pan frequently to prevent the discs sticking. Remove the first layer then continue the process by turning and peeling each layer until all five layers are removed easily.

5. While still hot cut each layer into a square by cutting the edges straight. Then cut the square into three equal strips. You should get 15 rectangles out of first batch. Place each on the working surface (a), and fold one third over (b). Paste the top third with flour and water paste then fold over the next third on top(c). You have a diamond shaped figure.

6. Put enough filling into the triangle base and seal the top two sides with flour and water paste (d). Use the paste liberally to ensure that the samosa is well sealed, otherwise it will burst while cooking.

7. Deep-fry the samosa at medium heat for about 10 minutes, or until light brown in colour. Don't over-cook or cook on too high a temperature. Let them get cold. You can freeze them at this stage.

8 To cook from frozen, grill on low temperature until piping hot or bake in the oven covered with foilk for 20-30 minutes at Gas Mark 4/180C/350F.

Makes 30 samosas.

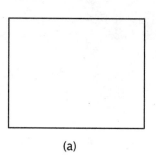 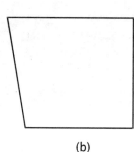 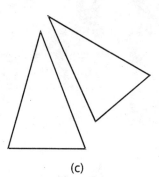 

   (a)   (b)   (c)   (d)

Mince Cutlets

Ingredients

1 lb/ 450g mince (beef or mutton)
3 onions
2 green chillies
1 inch piece of ginger
6 cloves of garlic
one bunch of coriander leaves
1 teaspoon pepper powder
1 egg
2 slices of bread (soaked in milk and drained)
Salt to taste
1 tablespoon of vinegar

Method

1. Mince the onions, green chillies, ginger, garlic and coriander.

2. Add the mixture to the minced meat with seasoning, egg and soaked bread.

3. Add vinegar and form into cutlets. Coat them in breadcrumbs and shallow fry.

Meat Samosa

Ingredients

For pastries:

Corn oil
1 lb (450g) strong white plain flour

For Filling:

1 teaspoon garam masala
2 large onions
1 lb (450g) lean minced meat
1 lb (450g) frozen peas
2 green chillies
2 tablespoon vinegar
1 teaspoon turmeric
1 teaspoon cumin powder
2 teaspoon chilli powder
salt to taste
2 teaspoon ground coriander powder

Method

1. Make the dough as specified in Vegetable Samosa and leave to rest.

2. Heat a little corn oil in a saucepan and fry the mince until brown. Cook the meat until all the juices are absorbed.

3. Add to the saucepan the onions, a little oil, chillies and salt and cook uncovered until the onions are soft. Then add all spice powders and simmer gently for about 25 minutes. The mixture should be fairly dry then add peas and cook for five minutes. Any liquid should be strained off. Leave it to cool.

4. Follow the same instructions for Vegetable Samosas.

Mince Potato Chops

Ingredients

1 kg potatoes
½ teaspoon pepper
salt to taste
1 egg slightly beaten
breadcrumbs
prepare mince as in
meat samosas shown on page 37

Method

1. Boil the potatoes in their skins until soft.

2. Peel and mash the potatoes.

3. Take a handful of potato mash and place it in the palm of your hand and hollow it a little, then put in some mince. Cover it with the mash to form a round shape or rectangle.

4. Dip into the egg mixture and then breadcrumbs.

5. Fry in shallow oil.

Portuguese Mince Patties

This recipe can be used with mince meat or fish. The patties can be frozen and deep-fried as and when required.

Ingredients

9 oz / 255 g of plain flour
1 tablespoon of corn flour
1 tablespoon of ghee or margarine
3 fl oz of water
Prepare mince as in meat samosas on page 37
2 tablespoon of oil

Method

1. Mix the flour with margarine or ghee and little salt
2. Add water a little at a time and knead into smooth dough.
3. Beat the dough with a wooden spoon till very smooth.
4. Divide the dough into four parts.
5. Take one part of the dough in your hand and make a small ball. Roll into a chapatti.
6. Brush the chapatti with oil generously and sprinkle a little cornflour.
7. Roll the chapatti tightly to form a roll. Stretch the roll to 8 inches.
8. Divide the roll into 6 equal portions.
9. Roll out each portion and put in a little mince. Seal it with a little water on the outer edges of the pastry to form a patty (can be of any shape i.e. rectangle, square or triangle).
10. Ensure the two ends are sealed firmly.
11. Continue the process till all the dough is finished.
12. Lastly, deep-fry the patties all together.

Croquettes

Ingredients

1 kg minced mutton or beef
3 onions finely chopped
4 green chillies deseeded and cut finely
½ teaspoon cloves powder
¼ tsp ginger paste
1 ½ tsp garlic paste
2 slices of bread
2 eggs
1 cup water
Half a cup of breadcrumbs
Oil for frying
Salt and pepper to taste

Method

1. Mix the mince, onions, chillies, garlic and ginger paste, salt and pepper with a cup of water.
2. Put the mixture in the pan and bring it to boil on a moderate heat and stir cook till all the water has been absorbed and the meat is dry.
3. Place the meat mixture in the blender and grind it finely. Soak the bread in milk for five minutes. Squeeze dry and add to the meat mixture along with 1 egg, lightly beaten.
4. Form the meat into the shape of cocktail sausages.
5. Beat the remaining egg and dip each croquette into the beaten egg, then into the breadcrumbs.
6. Heat the oil in a frying pan on a moderate heat and fry the croquettes to a golden brown colour. You should get about 30-35 croquettes.

Cleaning the mussels at home can be difficult and a tedious task. In Goa, the fisher-folks who sell these mussels clean them for their customers. Clean the mussels thoroughly to get rid of grit or sand. Once the mussels are removed from the shells they should not be washed, as the flavour will be lost.

Ingredients

12 large mussels in shells
2 Kashmiri dried chillies
3 cloves of garlic
1 onion finely sliced
½ inch piece ginger
¼ teaspoon garam masala
¼ tsp cumin seed powder
½ teaspoon sugar
1½ tablespoon of oil for cooking

Method

1. Wash and clean the mussels thoroughly. Remove the tiny bunch of hairs in each of them. With a sharp knife, prise open the shell and discard the empty half.

2. Wash and dry thoroughly 12 half empty shells to be used later.

3. Apply salt to the mussels and keep aside.

4. Grind all the spices in vinegar then add the garam masala, cumin powder, sugar and salt if required.

5. Marinate the mussels in the ground spices for 2 hours. Heat the oil in a pan on a moderate heat. Fry the onions until soft and add the mussels. Stir-fry for 10 minutes till well cooked and soft.

6. In each half shell place a mussel, and decorate with a sprig of coriander.

Fofos de Cavalas - Mackerel cutlets

This is a traditional Goan appetizer. During the fish season this recipe is widely used. It is cheap and simple to make. The recipe can be adapted to other white fish, such as cod and halibut, which are not available in Goa.

Ingredients

3 small mackerels cooked in
½ cup of water, cooled and flaked.
Reserve the fish stock to moisten
the fish mixture.
1 large egg, white and yolk separated
2 medium size onions, finely chopped
2 medium size potatoes, boiled and mashed
½ teaspoon of garlic
1 green chilli de-seeded and finely chopped
2 tbsp corn flour mixed with little fish stock
salt and pepper to taste
1 tsp juice of lemon
oil for deep frying
breadcrumbs for coating

Method

1. In a large bowl combine all the ingredients, except the egg white and oil.

2. Beat the egg white till stiff.

3. Form these rolls in different shapes, either round, finger shaped or rectangle.

4. Heat the oil in a deep frying pan.

5. Dip the fofos in the egg white and coat them in breadcrumbs, then deep fry to a golden brown colour.

These little turnovers can be served as appetisers. It is advisable to make in bulk and store them in the freezer to be deep-fried as and when required. They keep for couple of months.

Ingredients

For Pastry:

240g / 2 cups white plain flour
1 pt / 2 cups water
½ tsp salt
1 tbsp butter

For Filling:

450g / 1 cup shelled prawns,
cleaned and de-veined
2 tbsp oil
1½ cup finely chopped onions
2 green chillies, de-seeded and chopped
½ teaspoon of garlic paste
4 fl oz / ½ cup water
salt and pepper to taste
1 tbsp corn flour
1 tbsp grated cheese
oil for deep-frying
1 egg, lightly beaten
breadcrumbs for coating

Method

1. Sieve the flour.
2. Place water in a pan with salt and bring it to the boil. Add the butter, lower the heat and add the flour.
3. Stir and beat to mix till it forms a ball.
4. Remove from the heat and allow to cool – enough to handle. Knead well.
5. Chop the prawns finely.
6. Heat 2 tablespoons of vegetable oil in the pan and fry the onions, chillies and garlic till onions are transparent.
7. Add the prawns and cook till they turn light pink. Stir in water, salt and pepper and cook for 2 minutes.
8. Mix the cornflower with a little water and stir into the mixture. Cook till thick and creamy. Remove from the heat and add the cheese. Mix well and allow cooling.
9. Roll out pastry about 1/8 in thick. Cut out rounds about 2 inches in diameter.
10. Place one teaspoon filling on each round, fold over and moisten with water to seal. You should get approximately 40 rissois.
11. Heat the oil in a deep frying pan. Dip rissois in the beaten egg; roll in breadcrumbs and deep fry.
12. Drain on the paper towel and serve hot.

Stuffed eggs with Sausage meat

Ingredients

4 hard boiled eggs
¼ teaspoon freshly milled black pepper
6 spring onions cut finely
3 rashers of bacon cut finely and fried crisp
1lb /500g sausage meat
1 egg beaten slightly
1 tablespoon tomato sauce
1 tablespoon mayonnaise sauce
1 green chilli
Vegetable oil for frying
Salt and pepper to taste

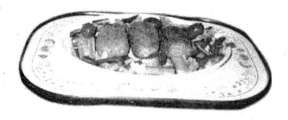

Method

1. Cut the eggs into halves (lengthwise)
2. Separate the yolks and place them in a bowl. Reserve the boiled egg whites in a separate bowl.
3. Cut the bacon rashers finely and fry them till crisp. Mix the onions, egg yolks, chilli, mayonnaise, tomato sauce, salt and pepper to form a smooth paste. Divide the sausage meat into eight equal portions.
4. Place a handful of sausage meat in the palm of your hand. Make it hollow and place the half of the outer coating of the boiled egg white in the middle. Fill it with the mixture and cover it with the sausage meat.
5. Dip in the beaten egg mixture and sprinkle with breadcrumbs.
6. Fry in shallow oil until golden brown.

Spinach and Rice Bhajas

These snacks are alternative to onion and potato bhajas and are wholesome and nutritious. Left over rice can be utilised.

Ingredients

250g green spinach
1 tsp olive oil
2 cups of almost soft cooked rice
1 cup of cooked lentils
6 oz of gram flour
2 onions finely chopped
6 oz of water
2 green chillies
1 tsp of spice No.3 on page 25
1 tbsp coriander powder
Vegetable oil for deep frying
Salt to taste

Method

1. Make the batter of gram flour with water. Add salt, spice and coriander powder. Mix thoroughly. Allow the batter to rest for half an hour or more.
2. Boil the spinach with olive oil. Strain all the liquid and leave it to cool. Mix the spinach, cooked rice, lentils, green chillies and onions. The consistency of the mixture should be solid.
3. Form the mixture into small balls, the size of table tennis ball.
4. Put vegetable oil in the wok or a deep frying pan. Bring it to the boiling point. Lower the heat to a medium temperature.
5. Dip the prepared balls in the batter and deep fry until they turn crisp and golden brown in colour.

Peixe enroladas - Rolled fish fillets

Skate, kingfish and baby sharks are available during fish season in Goa. They are cheap and plentiful. These fillets can be served with fried potato chips, green peas and green salad. This recipe can be used with green chilly and coriander paste on page 28.

Ingredients

½ kg fillet of shark or skate fish
2 tbsp vinegar or lime juice
2 tbsp of chilly and coriander paste or 2 tbsp rechear masala (see pgs 28 and 30 respectively)
oil for deep frying
1 egg, beaten
Semolina or bread crumbs for coating rolls

Method

1. Sprinkle the fish fillet with the vinegar or lime juice and salt. Leave it to marinate for one hour.

2. Apply the rechear masala or chilli and coriander paste on one side of each fillet. Roll carefully inwards and secure with cocktail sticks.

3. Heat the oil in a deep frying pan. Dip the fish rolls in beaten egg, roll in semolina or breadcrumbs and deep fry. Drain on paper towel.

4. Remove cocktail sticks and serve hot.

Prawn Fritters

Ingredients

1 large onion finely chopped
500 gm small cooked prawns, shelled
85 gm/3 oz self-raising flour
1 tsp baking powder
90 gm/3oz semolina flour
85 gm/3oz of rice flour
1tbs corn flour
1 inch thin sliced ginger, finely chopped
3 spring onions, finely chopped
½ red capsicum (pepper) , finely chopped
90 gm/3oz gram flour
¼ tbs turmeric
½ tsp ground cumin
¼ tsp chilli powder
1 tsp coriander
2 eggs, beaten
¾ pt water
1 tsp salt
250 ml oil for frying

Method

1. Combine self-raising flour, corn flour, baking powder, semolina flour, rice and gram flour in a bowl. Add beaten eggs and sufficient water to make thick batter. Then add the prawns and all the other ingredients. Mix well. Allow to stand for half an hour.

2. Heat the oil in a deep pan over moderate heat. Drop tablespoon of batter, a few at a time, into the oil and fry on both sides until golden brown. Drain the fritters on the kitchen paper . Garnish with coriander leaves. Serve hot with tomato sauce as a dip.

CHICKEN DISHES

This is another unique and mouth-watering dish that my aunt prepared for her family. You can substitute pork or veal for the chicken if you prefer.

Ingredients

1.5 kg/ 3lb 3oz whole chicken
2 large onions chopped
2-3 tablespoons vegetable oil
1 tsp ginger paste
2 fresh green chillies, chopped (optional)
4 fl oz / ½ cup of Goa vinegar
4 cloves of garlic, finely chopped
Salt to taste

Spices

½ teaspoon cloves powder
½ teaspoon cassia bark ground
½ teaspoon turmeric powder
½ teaspoon chilli powder
1 tsp coriander powder

Method

1. Joint the chicken into eight pieces.
2. Fry the onions until they are transparent, then add the garlic and ginger and simmer for 2 minutes.
3. Mix the spices with water to make a smooth paste. Add to the onion mixture and saute for two minutes. Add a little water if it gets too dry. Keep stirring.
4. Meanwhile fry the chicken pieces in a separate pan in the remaining oil, until the pieces are browned (for about 10 minutes).
5. Place the onion mixture and the chicken into a casserole dish, add the vinegar, chillies, salt and a little water and cook in the preheated oven at Gas Mark 4 / 180C/350F for 45 minutes or until the chicken is tender.

Jordan's Chicken in Green Masala

My cousin Jordan prepares this delicious chicken dish. The same ingredients can be used to make beef in green masala.

Ingredients

500 gm of boneless chicken
½ tsp salt
1 teaspoon of garlic and ginger paste on page 29
1 tbsp of lemon juice
2 green chillies
1 teaspoon of mint leaves
1 tsp of Spice No. 2 on page 24
2 tbsp oil
1 tbsp of curd or yogurt
2 tbsp chopped coriander
1 medium size onion (chopped)

Method

1. Cut the chicken into large cubes. Apply the salt, garlic and ginger paste and lemon juice and set aside.
2. Grind the chillies, parsley and mint into a smooth paste, then mix the curd and Spice No. 2.
3. Fry the onion to a light brown colour, then add the chicken pieces and fry for 2 minutes.
4. Mix the green masala paste with a little water and fry until the meat is well coated.
5. Continue to simmer until the meat is well cooked. If you prefer a little gravy then add two tablespoon of water.
6. Sprinkle with chopped coriander and serve with boiled potatoes and mixed vegetables.

Anne Mascarenhas' Chicken Curry

My friend Anne, who has now immigrated to Canada, gave me this recipe. My daughter liked the flavour very much, so much that I would prepare the dish quite often for my children when they were young.

Ingredients

Chicken (1kg/2.4 lb)
2 large onions
½ in piece of ginger
1 tsp cumin powder
½ teaspoon turmeric
½ teaspoon of cinnamon powder
small bunch of coriander leaves (chopped)

1 teaspoon coriander powder
8 small cloves of garlic
2 large tomatoes
2 teaspoon chilli powder
½ teaspoon of ground cloves
1 teaspoon tomato puree
2 tbsp of oil

Method

1. Cut the chicken into eight pieces.
2. Fry the onions in oil until golden brown. Add the chicken pieces and fry for about five minutes.
3. Grind the ginger and garlic to a smooth paste and mix with other spices and tomato puree, except the cloves and cinnamon.
4. Add the spices to the fried chicken pieces with a cup of hot water. Bring to the boil.
5. Cover the saucepan with the lid and simmer it on a low heat for 15 minutes.
6. Lastly add the cloves, cinnamon and chopped coriander leaves and cook for further two minutes.

Regina's Masala Combi (Spiced Chicken)

This is my sister-in-law's recipe. This is an easy yet delicious dish to prepare; the chicken is first boiled with spices, then fried with onions. Serve with chapattis and natural yoghurt.

Ingredients

1(kg/ 2.2lb) chicken
2 large onions
1 in piece of fresh root ginger
2 cloves garlic
salt to taste
1½ cups water
2 tbsp oil

1 teaspoon garam masala
1 teaspoon ground coriander
1 teaspoon ground cumin
2 teaspoons lemon juice
Chilli powder to taste
½ teaspoon turmeric powder

Method

1. Cut the chicken into eight pieces or leave whole if preferred. Grind one onion, the ginger and garlic to a smooth paste.
2. Place the chicken in a large pan along with the salt, chilli powder, turmeric, garam masala, coriander and cumin. Add the onion paste and lemon juice and pour in the water.
3. Bring it to the boil, lower the heat then simmer uncovered, over a very low heat until the chicken is tender and almost all the moisture has been absorbed.
2. Remove the chicken from the pan and set it aside, then slice thinly the remaining onion.
3. Heat the oil, add the onion and cooked chicken and fry it turning the chicken frequently, until both chicken and onions are golden in colour. Serve immediately. Alternatively, place the lightly fried onion and chicken under the grill for about 3-4 minutes turning on both sides.

Chicken Amsol - Sweet and sour chicken with tamarind juice

This is my family's favourite dish. It is so simple to prepare and yet it is delicious.

Ingredients

1.5 kg whole chicken cut into pieces as required
1 tablespoon of oil
6 large cloves of garlic crushed into smooth paste
4 dried red chillies, de-seeded and broken into two or three pieces
3 or 4 dried mango solam (mango slices)
2 bindi solam (optional)
1 tbs dried tamarind soaked in a half cup of warm water)
½ teaspoon salt
½ teaspoon sugar
4 fl oz of water

Method

1. Apply the salt to the chicken and leave it aside.

2. Heat the oil in the saucepan, add the garlic paste and chicken pieces.

3. Stir the chicken pieces to coat with the garlic paste. Cover the saucepan with the lid and simmer it on a low heat for about 5 minutes, stirring it occasionally. Uncover the saucepan and continue cooking until all the water is absorbed and the chicken is browned.

4. Squeeze the tamarind with your fingers to get all the pulp out of it. Now add the tamarind pulp, water, dried chillies, sugar, mango and bindi solam. Cook the chicken uncovered until most of the juice is absorbed and little gravy is left.

Chicken with Mustard, Honey and Coriander

Ingredients

3 breasts of chicken
1 tsp Dijon mustard paste ·
1 tbsp honey
1 tbsp chilli and coriander paste (pg 28)
1 tbsp lemon juice
salt and freshly milled pepper
1 tbsp plain flour
1 tsp corn flour
Vegetable oil for shallow frying
Breadcrumbs for coating

Method

1. Slice each chicken breast into half and sprinkle with the salt and freshly milled pepper.

2. In a small bowl put the honey, mustard paste, lemon juice, chilli and coriander paste and mix thoroughly. Apply the mixture to the chicken and marinate for an hour.

3. Make the batter of plain and corn flour.

4. Dip the chicken slices in the batter then roll in the breadcrumbs. Fry each side until they turn golden brown in colour.

Chicken Curry with Coconut Milk

This recipe can be substituted with beef on the bone.

Ingredients

1kg / 2lb 2 oz chicken cut into medium size pieces
½ teaspoon pepper powder
½ teaspoon turmeric powder
1 onion finely sliced
½ tsp cumin powder
¼ cinnamon powder
3 green chillies
1 tsp garlic paste
1 tsp ginger paste
1 tablespoon of Goa vinegar,
1 tbsp tamarind
4 fl oz of warm water
Salt to taste
6 fl oz thick coconut milk

Method

1. Apply the salt to the chicken pieces and leave aside
2. Grind all the spices, green chillies and tamarind with little water to form a paste then mix all the powdered spices.
3. Fry the onion till golden brown then add the garlic and ginger paste and fry briefly.
4. Add the chicken pieces followed by the ground masala and mix thoroughly.
5. Cover the pan and cook, when the water has evaporated allow the chicken pieces to fry well.
6. Add warm water to the chicken pieces and cook uncovered for about 10 minutes.
7. Add the coconut milk and simmer till the gravy is thickened.
8. Lastly add the vinegar and simmer for a couple of minutes.

Chicken Breasts with Sherry

Ingredients

2 chicken breasts (weighing 500g)
2 tbsp olive oil
2 red peppers chopped
1 onion chopped
2 cloves of garlic minced
2 large tomatoes peeled and cut coarsely
100 ml sherry wine
100 ml water
15 stuffed olives
Salt and pepper

Method

1. Cut the chicken breasts in half, making four fillets. Flatten them slightly.
2. Heat the oil in a frying pan and fry the chicken breasts lightly on both sides, without browning, turning only once.
3. In the same oil sauté the chopped onions and peppers until softened. Add the chopped garlic and tomatoes. Fry for a few minutes then add the sherry, water, salt and pepper.
4. Cook on a medium heat for about 12-15 minutes.
5. Return the chicken breasts to the frying pan and cook on a low heat for about 10-15 minutes.
6. Transfer to a serving dish and garnish with the sliced olives. Serve with green salad and boiled potatoes.

These chicken chops are delicious with boiled potatoes and fresh green salad or side vegetable dishes.

Ingredients

1 lb (450g) boneless chicken, preferably breasts of chicken
1 teaspoon of olive oil
2 green chillies chopped
2 tablespoon of fresh coriander washed and chopped
½ teaspoon salt
1 tablespoon of lemon juice or vinegar
½ tsp freshly milled pepper

Method

1. Cut each breast of chicken into three slices and sprinkle with salt and freshly milled pepper.

2. Put the green chillies, fresh coriander, lemon juice and olive oil in the blender and blend it into a smooth paste.

3. Apply the paste to the chicken and marinate for couple of hours or more. The longer you keep it the better it will taste.

4. Pre-heat the grill and spread the chicken on the oven tray and cook at a moderate heat for approximately 15 minutes. At half time turn the chicken and cook until it is tender and juicy.

Goan Piri-Piri Chicken

This is Portugal's national dish; it was widely eaten in Goa during the Portuguese occupation. The chicken is sautéed with dry low alcohol wine, which has a tangy flavour (vinho verde is preferable) and small fiery chillies to bring out the exotic flavour.

Ingredients

4 chicken breasts, skinned and boned
3 garlic cloves
1 small onion finely chopped
2 red chillies
2 red peppers
3 tbsp olive oil
200ml or 7 fl oz dry white wine (Vinho verde)
Salt and black pepper
1 tbsp fresh coriander chopped
1 teaspoon of tomato puree
½ teaspoon of sugar

Method

1. Cut the chicken breasts into thin strips. Finely chop the garlic. Cut the chillies and peppers in half, remove the seeds and all the white pith. Cut both into thin strips.

2. Heat half the oil in a large pan, add the chicken strips and stir-fry over a high heat, stirring all the time, for a couple of minutes or until slightly browned. Remove the chicken from the pan and set aside.

3. Add the rest of the oil to the pan, add the garlic, chillies, onion and peppers and fry for about 3 minutes or until softened. Add the wine and bring to the boil. Return the chicken to the pan, seasoned with salt and pepper. Reduce the heat to moderately low, cover the pan and simmer for 15 minutes.

4. While the chicken is cooking, cut the coriander leaves finely and sprinkle the chicken with coriander and serve.

This dish is very popular and delicious to eat. It is usually very hot and sour. For milder effect use less chilli powder. It goes well with boiled rice and green salad.

Ingredients

1 kg chicken pieces
60g butter or margarine
1 tsp ground mustard
1 ½ tsp turmeric powder
30ml / 1fl oz water
2 medium size onions sliced
1 tsp garlic paste
1 tsp ginger paste
1 inch cinnamon stick
1 ½ chilli powder
1 ½ tsp cumin powder
½ tsp salt
1 tbsp sugar
4 cloves
2 tbsp white vinegar
1 tsp tomato puree

Method

1. Place all the spices, the vinegar and the sliced onion in a blender or food processor. Blend the ingredients into a smooth paste.

2. Apply the spice mixture and the sugar to the chicken pieces and marinate for about six hours or preferably overnight.

3. Fry the sliced remaining onion in the melted butter until they are transparent. Add the marinated chicken pieces, water and the tomato puree, cover the saucepan and simmer on a low heat for about 40 minutes, stirring occasionally or until the chicken is tender.

Spring Roll Pastry

Ingredients

250g /8 oz plain flour
2 tbsp oil
½ tsp salt.

Method

1. Put the plain flour in a bowl with the salt. Rub in the oil and mix the dough well.

2. Add enough warm water to make a soft dough.

3. Knead well for 5 minutes.

4. Cover and allow to rest for 30 minutes.

5. Divide the dough into 3 portions. Roll out each portion very thinly to form a pastry.

6. Cut the pastry into squares. Use the squares to make Spring rolls shown in recipe on pg 61. Keep the remaining dough covered.

Sweet and Fruity Chicken Curry

Mango and pineapple are plentiful in Goa and this dish is sweet and fruity and can be served with rice or chapattis. It is ideal for young children.

Ingredients

4 boneless breasts of chicken
1 tbsp plain flour
½ teaspoon salt
7 fl oz chicken stock
4 fl oz natural yoghurt
6 shallots cut into fine slices
½ teaspoon of chilli powder
½ teaspoon turmeric
1 teaspoon of cumin
¼ teaspoon of cinnamon
1 tbsp of coriander leaves chopped
1 half ripened mango peeled and cut into cubes
½ fresh pineapple peeled and cut into small cubes
4 cloves powdered finely
1 in fresh ginger finely chopped
2 tbsp grated coconut
2 tbsp vegetable oil or ghee
2 tbsp coriander to garnish

Method

1. Cut the chicken breasts into 1 inch long strips. Mix the chicken strips with flour, salt and pepper to cover evenly.
2. Heat the oil in a large frying pan or wok. Shake off any excess flour from the chicken and add the strips to the pan. Fry for 5 minutes over a high heat or until browned. Remove from the pan with a slotted spoon and set aside.
3. Fry the shallots and ginger in the pan for 2 minutes. Mix all the spices with little water and add to the pan with the fruit. Fry for about 1 minute on a low heat, stirring. Add chicken stock and bring it to the boil. Lower the heat and simmer for 5 minutes. Return the chicken and stir in the yoghurt. Season if required. Cover and simmer on a very low heat for a further 5 minutes.
4. Meanwhile, fry the grated coconut in a frying pan over a high heat. Sprinkle over the curry before serving. Garnish with the chopped coriander.

Goan Roast Chicken

Ingredients

1 kg/ 2 lb.2oz whole chicken (giblets removed)
8 peppercorns
4 cloves
1 x 1 in cinnamon stick
½ tsp ginger paste
1 tsp garlic paste
2 cardamoms
salt to taste
juice of one lemon
5 fluid oz of water

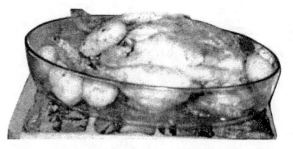

Method

1. Apply the salt and lemon juice and allow to marinate for two hours.
2. Place the chicken in the saucepan with all the spices, lemon juice and water. Bring it to the boil. Cover the saucepan with the lid and simmer on a low heat for 20 minutes.
3. Remove the chicken and save the stock for gravy.
4. Preheat the oven on Gas Mark 4 /180C/350F and cook the chicken for about 45 minutes or until it is golden brown in colour. Remove the chicken from the oven and cover it with foil to keep it warm.
5. Strain the stock and cook on high heat till the sauce is thickened. Adjust the seasoning. Serve with boiled or roast potatoes. .

This is a Chinese dish. It can be prepared with pork, chicken or vegetables. These rolls can be served with Chilly sauce. Instead of buying readymade spring roll wrappers, you can prepare them as indicated in recipe 'Spring Roll Pastry'.

Ingredients

3 tbsp oil
250 g /8 oz lean pork or breast chicken.
250 g bean sprouts rinsed out
4 spring onions
2 tbsp mushrooms, fresh or dry Chinese mushrooms soaked in hot water for half an hour
2 oz cooked prawns
1 coarsely grated carrot
1 inch slice ginger chopped finely
1 clove garlic chopped finely
1½ tsp dark soy sauce
1 tsp salt
10 spring roll wrappers, defrosted
2 tbsp flour mixed with 1 tbsp water (to make a paste for sealing)
oil for deep frying

Method

1. Cut the meat or chicken into matchstick-long pieces.

2. Cut the spring onions into silver threads, slice the mushrooms finely, and chop the prawns.

3. Heat the oil in a wok, when hot adds the garlic, ginger and salt. Add the meat or chicken and stir-fry until cooked. Add the mushrooms, then carrots, spring onions, prawns and the bean shoots. Add the soy sauce and sugar. Toss well together. Do not overcook!

4. Transfer the contents of the wok into a colander, allow to drain whilst cooling. Throw away any liquid left over on the plate. When cool fill the wrappers with the mixture.

5. Divide the stuffing into 10 portions. Place each portion on the pastry just below the centre, fold the bottom half over the stuffing. Fold the right side towards the centre, do the same for the left side. The shape should look like an envelope.

6. Roll up into a tight roll, seal with the paste made with the flour and water.

7. Deep fry rolls for 2-3 minutes turning them over once. Remove them from the wok. Drain on absorbent paper.

Ingredients

4 chicken thighs boned, skinned and diced

A
{
3-4 tbsp of lingham's chilly sauce (Malaysian product)
1 tsp sugar
2 tsp lemon juice
}

B
{
1½ tsp corn flour
1 ½ tbsp light soy sauce
¼ tsp salt
½ tsp sugar
½ Tabasco sauce
}

C
{
1 tsp sesame oil
1 medium onion peeled and sliced
1 clove garlic crushed and chopped
4 cardamoms
4 cloves
1 –1 ½ inch cinnamon stick
1 inch length ginger root – crushed roughly or chopped
4 -5 pieces of star anise
}

Vegetable oil for shallow frying

Method

1. Get all the ingredients ready and prepare A, B and C in three separate bowls.
2. Season the chicken with B and blend with sesame oil. Allow to marinate for 15 minutes.
3. Heat the wok to a medium heat. Pour in the oil and bring it to the boil. Add in C and stir for 1-2 minutes. Mix in the garlic, stir, then add in the onions. Stir for further 2 minutes.
4. Add the marinated chicken and continue to cook on a moderate heat by stirring constantly for about 10 minutes.
5. When the chicken is almost ready, add in A and continue to cook by stirring until the chicken is well coated and cooked. Serve hot.

Ingredients

1.5 kg/ 3lbs whole chicken or chicken pieces, skinned and cut into large pieces (use preferably legs, thighs and breasts)
3 tbsp tandoori paste on page 29
salt to taste
juice of one lemon
2 tbsp vegetable oil
450ml /15 fl oz (plain) yoghurt beaten
1 lemon cut into wedges
1 medium red onion cut into rounds
1 ½ food colouring (optional)

Method

1. Remove the skin from the chicken and trim off any excess fat. Make several diagonal slits into the flesh of the chicken. Cut slits in the meaty side of each breast. Apply salt and lemon juice. Set aside.
2. Mix the yoghurt with the masala paste and the food colouring, if using.
3. Spread the chicken evenly with the yoghurt mixture, spreading some into the slits.
4. Leave to marinate for at least two hours or preferably overnight.
5. Warm the oil and pour over the chicken to seal the surface. Oil helps to keep the centre moist while roasting.
6. Pre-heat the oven Gas Mark 6 / 200C /400 F and cook in the oven for 20-25 minutes at maximum heat, then remove, leaving the oven on.
7. Baste the chicken pieces with the remaining marinade. Return to the oven and switch off the heat. Leave the chicken in the oven for about 15-20 minutes without opening the door. Serve on a bed of lettuce and garnish with the lemon wedges and sliced tomatoes.

Chicken Tikka Masala

The recipe for making Tandoori chicken is given above. To make chicken Tikka masala is simple and quick. The marinade and the cooking juices from Tandoori chicken are reserved for this dish, in addition to the ingredients shown below.

Ingredients

4 chicken pieces (1.5 kg / 3lbs)
4 tbsp of olive oil
6 cardamom pods
2 x 1 in piece of cinnamon
2 medium size onions finely chopped
2 tbsp garlic and ginger paste (pg 29)
1 tbsp ground coriander
1 tsp ground cumin
½ tsp turmeric powder
150 ml (4 fl oz) water
1 tsp red paprika powder
6 tbsp tandoori chicken marinade
1 tsp tomato puree
2 tbsp double cream
Salt to taste

Method

1. Put the oil in a large heavy saucepan or a wok and heat it over a medium heat. When the oil is very hot add the cardamom pods and cinnamon sticks, stir once, and then the add onions. Fry until they turn golden brown.
2. Now add the ginger and garlic paste and cook for a minute.
3. Mix all other spices with little water and make it into a smooth paste. Add to the pan and stir for a few seconds.
4. Add the tandoori chicken marinade, a little at a time, and stir it in, until all the marinade is used. Now add tomato puree and cook stirring for a minute. Then +
5. Cover the saucepan and lower the heat, simmer gently for about 10 minutes. Incorporate the cooked tandoori chicken pieces and any juices from the baking tray. Raise the heat to high and cook till the sauce is thickened and the chicken pieces are well coated.
6. Lastly, add the double cream and cook on low heat for 1 minute, stirring continuously.

My second son, Norman, first prepared this dish for his birthday party. The family enjoyed the dish so much that we all got the recipe from him and included in our repertoire. It has a hot and sweet flavour and a deep, characteristic, reddish brown colour.

Ingredients

1 lb or ½ kg chicken breast meat, skinned and boned.
½ teaspoon salt
1 tablespoon corn flour
2 tsp vegetable oil
4 spring onions
½ red pepper
2 small dried red chillies
1 lb can bamboo shoot pieces
2 tablespoons dry sherry
1 tablespoon sesame oil
sprigs of coriander, or parsley to garnish

The sauce:

2 cloves garlic crushed
1 tbsp soy bean paste
2 tbsp soy sauce
1 tbsp hoisin sauce
2 tbsp tomato puree
2 tsp sugar
4 tbsp chicken stock
½ tsp Tabasco sauce
vegetable oil for shallow frying

Method

1. Cut the chicken into 1 inch cubes. Sprinkle them with salt, corn flour and oil and rub it into the chicken with the fingertips.

2. Trim the spring onions and cut each into 3 pieces. Cut the red pepper into small dice. Cut off the stalk ends of the dried chillies and discard all the seeds.

3. Drain the canned bamboo shoots and cut into half.

4. Put all the sauce ingredients together in a small bowl. Mix well.

5. Pour enough oil in a large frying pan to give a depth of ¼ in. Heat the oil until it is very hot, and then add the chicken cubes, spreading them out flat in the pan.

6. Fry over a high heat for 3-4 minutes, turning them, until lightly golden. Remove them from the pan with a slotted spoon.

7. Allow the oil to cool a little, and then pour away all but 2 tablespoons of it. Re-heat the frying pan then add the spring onions, red pepper and whole dried chillies to the pan and stir-fry over a medium heat for 1 minute.

8. Add the sauce and stir over the heat until smooth. Add the bamboo shoots and stir-fry for 1 minute, until heated through and coated with the sauce.

9. Add the chicken and cook for a few seconds until just heated through. Finally stir in the sherry and sesame oil.

10. Transfer to a heated serving dish, garnish with sprigs of coriander and serve immediately.

Chicken with Almond Sauce

Ingredients

½ tsp coriander powder
½ tbsp ground almonds
150g Greek yoghurt, whipped
½ tsp garam masala powder
½ tsp cumin powder
1tsp turmeric powder
1 tbsp mild red chilli powder
1 tsp salt

1 tbsp lemon juice
12 chicken legs (weighing about 1 kg)
3 tbsp vegetable oil
2 medium size onions finely chopped
7 cloves garlic finely chopped
1 tsp ginger paste
3 fresh tomatoes, chopped
1 chicken stock cube

Method

1. In a mixing bowl, whip the yoghurt thoroughly and add the ground almond powder, other spice powders and lemon juice. Mix thoroughly, then marinate the chicken for 15 minutes.

2. Pre-heat the oven to Gas Mark 4, 180C or 350F.

3. In a large heavy saucepan, heat the oil, then add the onions, ginger and garlic and cook on a low heat for about 10 minutes until the onions are transparent and slightly brown in colour. Now add the tomatoes and crumbled chicken stock cube and cook for another 5 minutes to dry out the tomato moisture. Add the chicken and sauté for 5 minutes.

4. Remove the chicken from the heat. Put the chicken in the roasting tin and place it in the pre-heated oven to cook for approximately 50 minutes. Turn the oven off and leave the door shut for 15 minutes, this will allow the dish to rest. Stir well before serving . Serve with boiled rice, chapatti or slices of whole meal bread and steamed vegetables.

Chicken Biryani

Ingredients

500g/1/2 kg basmati rice
30ml/2tbsp vegetable oil
1 green chilli, finely chopped
4 cloves of garlic crushed
675g /1 ½ lb boneless chicken
1 ½ fresh root ginger
2 onions thinly sliced
45ml/3 3tbsp curry paste

1.5 ml / ½ salt
4 tomatoes cut into thin wedges
1.7m/ ½ tsp ground turmeric
5 cloves
3 bay leaves
1/7m / ½ tsp garam masala
5 green cardamom pods
1.5ml/ ¼ tsp saffron strands

Method

1. Wash the rice thoroughly in cold water. Place the rice in a large bowl with plenty of cold water and let it soak for 30 minutes.

2. In the meantime, heat the oil in the large frying pan and fry the onions until soft and lightly browned. Add the garlic, chilli and ginger and fry for about 2 minutes. Add the chicken and fry for about 6 minutes, stirring occasionally.

3. Add the curry paste, salt and garam masala and cook for about 5 - 6 minutes. Now add the tomatoes and continue to cook for a further 4 minutes. Remove from the heat and set aside.

4. Preheat the oven to 190 C/375F/Gas 5. Bring a large saucepan of water to the boil. Drain the rice and add it to the pan with the turmeric. Cook for about 10 minutes or the rice is almost ready. Drain the rice and toss together with the bay leaves, cardamoms, cloves and saffron.

5. In a shallow, ovenproof dish place cooked rice as first layer, then chicken mixture, continue using rice and chicken mixture until all the mixture has been used, finishing off with a layer of rice . Cover with a lid or foil and bake in the oven for 15-20 minutes, or until chicken is ready when pierced with the tip of a knife. Transfer to individual plates and serve with chutney.

Duck Curry

This is an authentic Indian dish, which is rich, spicy and easy to make. Serve it with plain boiled basmati rice and fresh green salad.

Ingredients

3 kg/ 6lbs duck cut into individual portions
salt to taste
4 medium sized onions, finely chopped
½ tsp garlic paste
1 tsp ginger paste
1 tsp mustard seeds
5 tbsp oil
1 tsp of cumin powder
1 green chilli finely chopped
2 large tomatoes, skinned, de-seeded and chopped finely
1 tsp chilli powder
1 tbsp garam masala
1 tsp turmeric
1 tbsp ground coriander
4 tbsp vinegar
12 fl oz (1½ cups of boiling water)
½ inch slice of creamed coconut
1 tsp sugar

Method

1. In a large heavy saucepan, heat the oil over a moderate heat. Add the duck pieces and fry them for 4 to 5 minutes on each side or until they are golden brown. Remove the pieces with a slotted spoon and set them aside on a plate.
2. Add the mustard seeds, cover the pan and fry them for a minute. Keep the pan covered or the mustard seeds will spatter. Remove the cover and add the onions, fry them until they are golden brown.
3. Add the garlic, ginger and green chillies and fry stirring constantly for about 2 minutes.
4. Mix with the vinegar, the cumin, chilli powder, coriander, garam masala, turmeric and salt, and then make it into a paste. Add the paste to the saucepan and fry, stirring constantly for couple of minutes.
5. Add the duck pieces and turn them over several times so that they are well coated with spices. Continue frying for 3 minutes.
6. In a small bowl, dissolve the creamed coconut in the water to make coconut milk. Pour the coconut milk over the duck pieces and stir to mix the coconut milk into the pieces.
7. Reduce the heat to moderately low, cover the pan and simmer for 40 minutes or until the duck is tender and the gravy is thick.
8. Taste the curry and adjust seasoning, by adding salt and sugar, if necessary.

Chilli Chicken

Ingredients

1 kg boneless chicken pieces
2 tbsp oil
½ tsp chilli powder
½ tsp ground paprika
1/8 tsp ground cinnamon
½ tsp ground turmeric

¼ tsp ground mustard
2 cloves garlic, crushed
2 tbsp plain yoghurt
1 large onion sliced in rings and soaked in lemon juice
1 tbsp fresh lemon juice

Method

1. Combine chilli, paprika, cloves, mustard, cinnamon, turmeric, garlic, yoghurt and lemon juice in a bowl. Add chicken and marinate for at least eight hours or preferably overnight.
2. Heat oil in a frying pan, add chicken in single layer, fry both sides until lightly browned. Transfer the chicken pieces and the sauce to an ovenproof dish.
3. Preheat the oven to Gas Mark 6/200C/400F and bake uncovered for 15 minutes or until the chicken is tender. Serve with rice and green salad.

PORK DISHES

Pork Amsol

This dish is very simple and cheap to make, yet it is delicious with rice or chapattis. The cooking method differs from chicken Amsol.

Ingredients

1 lb or 500g streaky slices of lean pork or pork belly (cut into small cubes)
1 small onion sliced finely
3 dried red chillies (broken into half and de-seeded]
5 cloves of garlic crushed into a smooth paste
½ teaspoon salt
2 dried mango solam (slices)
2 bindi solam
6 fl oz of water
½ tsp sugar
1 tablespoon vegetable oil
1 tsp tamarind soaked in 4 fluid ounces of warm water

Method

1. Place the pork, onion and salt in the pan and rub it with your hands by squeezing the juice of the onion into the meat.
2. Add the garlic, dried chillies, sugar, dried mango and bindi solam.
3. Soak the tamarind in the water and squeeze out all the juice by rubbing with your fingers, making sure that all the juice is extracted.
4. Add the tamarind juice to the pan and bring it to the boil.
5. Stir well and then add one tablespoon of oil.
6. Cover the saucepan with the lid and simmer it on a low fire for about 5 minutes. Adjust to taste by adding salt, sugar and warm water if required. Take the lid off and continue to simmer for further 15 minutes or until the meat is tender and juicy.

Aad Mass (Sang Sol) - Hot and Sour Pork Bone Meat Curry

The meat should be with bones, preferably pork ribs cut into small pieces. It is very tasty finger-licking dish. Serve with plain basmati rice.

Ingredients

1 kg / 2lb 2 oz pork ribs
1 ½ tsp chilli powder
1 cup water
1 tbsp tamarind soaked in half cup of warm water
½ tsp cumin powder
½ tsp turmeric powder
2 tsp ginger and garlic paste
1 large onion chopped finely
2 green chillies chopped finely
1 tbsp of oil
½ tsp sugar
salt to taste
3 cloves
1 inch cinnamon
1 tbs vinegar

Method

1. Fry the onion and green chillies until transparent.
2. Add the pork and simmer until water oozes out.
3. Add ginger and garlic paste then mix all the spice powders with little water to form the paste. Add to the pan and simmer for couple of minutes. Now add one cup of water and cook covered on a low heat for 30 minutes.
4. When the meat is tender, add the tamarind juice, vinegar and sugar. Cook for 10 minutes longer. The meat on the bone will almost disintegrate. It should be soft and juicy.

Loin Pork Steaks

This dish is delicious with boiled potatoes, carrots, cabbage or green salad. It goes well with mango chutney or apple sauce.

Ingredients

1 kg or 2lb 2oz of pork steaks (approx 5 loin pork steaks)
1 teaspoon of freshly milled ground pepper
2 cloves of garlic crushed into a smooth paste
½ inch ginger finely grated
salt to taste
juice of one lemon
½ teaspoon lemon zest

Method

1. Sprinkle salt and pepper on the meat

2. Add the garlic, ginger, lemon juice and lemon zest and leave it to rest in the fridge for couple of hours.

3. Cook under a medium grill for 12- 15 minutes, turning occasionally.

Pork Vindaloo - Spicy Pork Curry

Ingredients

1lb (500g) lean pork cut into 2 inches cubes
3 onions finely sliced
2 tbsp garlic and ginger paste (pg29)
8 Kashmiri chillies
½ teaspoon cumin seeds
6 cloves
½ tsp pepper powder
½ teaspoon turmeric powder
3 green chillies (sliced lengthwise)
1 teaspoon salt
1 teaspoon sugar
1 tbsp tamarind soaked in warm water
½ tsp mustard seeds

Method

1. Grind the garlic and ginger with vinegar into a smooth paste.

2. Put chillies, pepper, cumin and cloves into a food processor or blender and blend until the chillies are ground finely. Add the turmeric powder and half the quantity of garlic and ginger paste and mix well.

3. Fry the onions with the remaining garlic and ginger paste until light brown.

4. Add the pork, then the ground masala and fry for about 10 minutes.

5. Add warm water sufficient to cover the pork.

6. Simmer it until the gravy is reduced to half.

7. Add the green chillies, sugar and salt to taste.

8. With a little water dissolve the tamarind and add to the pan.

9. Continue to simmer on a low heat till the gravy is thickened.

Roast Pork (Goan Version)

Ingredients

1lb (450g) half leg of Pork
½ teaspoon turmeric
5 cloves of garlic
½ teaspoon ground pepper
1 inch ginger peeled
1 inch cinnamon
5 cloves
2 red whole chillies
1 tablespoon of Goa vinegar or malt vinegar
½ tsp salt
1½ tablespoons of vegetable oil.

Method

1. Sprinkle the salt on the meat and rub it well with your fingers.

2. Grind the ginger and garlic, mix the turmeric, vinegar and pepper and rub the mixture on to the meat.

3. Add all the other ingredients to the meat and allow to marinate for couple of hours.

4. Heat the oil in the pan and fry the pork till brown. Meanwhile pre-heat the oven. Cover the roast with foil and roast at Gas Mark 4/ 180 C /350 F for about 45 – 50 minutes or until the meat is tender.

Margaret's Glazed Ham

A friend gave this recipe to me and I have prepared this side dish several times for Christmas festivities, as one of the Christmas trimmings. It can be served hot or cold with roast turkey or chicken.

Ingredients

Piece of ham weighing 1 kg
A few cloves
2 level tablespoons of Demerara sugar
1 tsp dry mustard
2 tbsp of clear honey
1 tsp of ground cinnamon or ginger
¼ pint of cider or sherry wine
1 pint of water

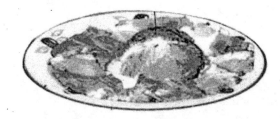

Method

1. Soak the ham in cold water for 3-4 hours. Drain the water.

2. Place the ham in the pan with the water and the skin side down. Bring slowly to the boil skimming off the scum.

3. Reduce the heat and cover with lid and simmer for half the cooking time at Gas Mark 4 /180C/ 350F for 20-25 minutes per 1 lb + 20 minutes.

4. Drain and remove the skin with a sharp knife. Score the fat with a criss-cross pattern. Stick cloves into each diamond space.

5. Mix the sugar, mustard, spice and honey. Put the joint into a roasting tin and spread the sugar mixtures over the scored fat and pour the remaining liquid around it.

6. Bake in the centre of the oven for the remaining cooking time, basting regularly.

Pork Assad

Ingredients

1lb/ 500g pork joint
1 inch ginger peeled
1 full pod of garlic peeled
½ teaspoon turmeric
½ tsp ground pepper
½ tsp salt
1 inch piece of cinnamon
3 whole red chillies
5 cloves
1 tablespoon of vegetable oil
1 ½ tbsp vinegar

Method

1. Tenderise the pork joint with a fork and sprinkle the salt all over.
2. Grind the ginger and garlic, add the turmeric and pepper, then rub the mixture on to the pork joint.
3. Heat the oil or ghee in the pan and fry the pork until it is brown.
4. Add 240ml or 8 fl oz of water, cinnamon, cloves, vinegar and red chillies (whole). Cover the pan with the lid and cook on moderate heat till the liquid is dry and the pork is tender.

Fried Pork Chops

Ingredients

1lb (450g) lean pork
2 green chillies
1 inch ginger
6 cloves of garlic
¼ tsp salt
6 peppercorns
½ tsp chilli powder
½ tsp. turmeric
1 egg
breadcrumbs

Method

1. Apply the salt to the meat and boil. Then cut into slices.
2. Grind the green chillies, ginger, garlic and peppercorns, and mix in the chilli powder and the turmeric.
3. Rub the mixture on to the boiled pork slices.
4. Beat the egg slightly and dip each slice in the egg mixture and cover it with breadcrumbs and fry.Gammon Steaks with Honey and Mustard

Gammon Steaks with Honey and Mustard

Ingredients

3 gammon steaks weighing 500g
6 peppercorns
½ tsp mustard paste
1" cinnamon stick
4 cloves
1 tbsp honey
1 bay leaf
2 fl oz water

Method

1. Place the gammon, honey, water and spices in the saucepan and bring it to the boil. Simmer for 10-12 minutes. Drain and set aside.
2. Sprinkle on freshly ground pepper and coat with honey. Then grill for couple of minutes on each side.
3. Serve with green salad, sliced tomatoes and boiled potatoes.

53

This dish was Ti-Pedro's pork speciality. My uncle Pedro slaughtered a pig on a feast day. He would sell most of the meat with the exception of these delicacies. He would then prepare this mouth-watering dish for his family.   It consisted of all the delicacies of a reasonably young pig such as pork liver, heart, tongue, kidneys, stomach, and the meat of the upper part of the neck of the pigling.   This dish is somewhat similar to sorpatel. In Goa you can buy a batch of these delicacies if you order in advance from the local seller of pork meat.

Ingredients

1kg / 2lb 2oz pork of the upper part of the neck of the young pig or pigling
1 pork liver 1 tongue and 1 heart
2 kidneys
Stomach
½ cup blood of the pig
1 cup water
1 teaspoon sugar
salt to taste
¼ cup oil
2 medium size onions
2 tablespoon of Goa feni (optional)
2 green chillies, de-seeded and slit into two slices

Spices to grind:

10 Kashmiri chillies de-seeded
8 peppercorns
12 cloves garlic
1 inch piece of ginger
1 teaspoon cumin seeds
8 cloves
2 x 1" piece of cinnamon
¾ cup vinegar

Method

1. Wash and drain the meat thoroughly. Pat the meat dry. Cut it into small cubes. Apply salt to taste and leave it to rest for half an hour.

2. Grind all the spices in vinegar.

3. Apply the ground paste to the meat and keep aside for half a day to marinate.

4. Heat the oil in a deep pan on medium heat and fry the onions until transparent. Remove the onions from the pan and set aside. In the same oil stir-fry the spiced meat for about 10 to 15 minutes. Now add the green chillies, feni, sugar, water and blood.

5. Mix thoroughly. Bring it to the boil

6. Lower the heat and cook for an hour, stirring occasionally.

7. Adjust the seasoning, by adding sugar, salt and vinegar, if necessary.

8. Like sorpatel this dish tastes better if it is re-heated for three days continuously. It is ready to be served on the fourth day.

Pork Trotters Curry

It is a favourite dish of my husband. You can ask the butcher to cut the trotters according to the size you wish to have.

Ingredients

1 dozen trotters cut into sizeable pieces
4 red chillies
½ tsp turmeric powder
1 tablespoon coriander seeds
2 green chillies cut lengthwise
1 inch ginger
10 cloves of garlic
salt to taste
1 tbsp tamarind soaked in 4 fl oz of water
1 tablespoon of oil
1½ cup water
1 tsp cumin seeds

Method

1. Wash the trotters well, then dip in the boiling water. Scrape off any hair left with the knife.

2. Boil them in salted water till tender or put in the pressure cooker for about 10-15 minutes.

3. Grind the red chillies, turmeric, cumin, coriander, ginger and six cloves of garlic.

4. Crush the remaining cloves of garlic and fry in oil, add the ground masala and fry again.

5. Put in the trotters along with the water in which they have been cooked and simmer till almost dry.

6. Add tamarind juice and adjust seasoning. Add green chillies and simmer till the meat is dropping of the bones.

Porco com Arroz - Pork Pullau (Portuguese style)

This dish is cooked with Basmati rice rather than local rice found in Goa. It can be cooked in different number of ways by combining with meat, shellfish (prawns, shrimps) or vegetables. The dishes are satisfying and nutritious, needing nothing more than salad as an accompaniment.

Ingredients

2 tablespoon olive oil
1 large onion, finely chopped
1 clove garlic chopped
1 lb / 500g lean, boneless pork cut into small pieces
12 oz / 1½ cup basmati rice
3 cups chicken stock
salt & freshly ground pepper
½ teaspoon turmeric powder
a pinch of saffron threads, mixed with 1 tablespoon of warm milk.
2 x 1" sticks of cinnamon broken into half
4 cloves

Method

1. Heat the oil in a large heavy saucepan and sauté the onion, then add the garlic and pork continue frying until the onion is soft and pork is lightly brown.

2. Add the rice and cook, stirring over a low heat for about 3 minutes or until all the grains are cooked with oil.

3. Pour in the stock, season with salt and pepper, saffron mixture and cinnamon. Bring it to the boil.

4. Cover the pan and simmer over a low heat for 15 minutes to blend the flavours. Allow to stand for 5 minutes before serving.

This is a great Portuguese dish served in Goa without its original name. Calf's or lamb's liver can be used, if preferred.

Ingredients

6 fl ounces of dry white wine
1 tablespoon white wine vinegar
4 cloves garlic chopped
1 bay leaf
salt and freshly ground pepper
1 lb pork, calf's or lamb's liver, thinly sliced
2 ounces (4 slices) bacon chopped
3 tablespoons oil

Method

1. In a bowl combine the wine, vinegar, garlic, bay leaf, salt and pepper to taste.
2. Add the liver and marinate in the refrigerator overnight.
3. When ready to cook, lift out and dry the liver.
4. Heat the oil in a frying pan and sauté the bacon until crisp.
5. Add the liver and cook over a moderate heat for 1 minute on each side (if using pork liver) or 30 seconds on each side for calf's or lamb's liver.
6. Lift out the liver and bacon on to a warm serving dish, cover and keep warm.
7. Remove and discard the bay leaf from the marinade. Pour the marinade into the pan, bring it to boil over a high heat and reduce it to about half.
8. Pour over the liver and serve with sliced boiled potatoes, sprinkled with chopped coriander.

Char-siu – Chinese Roast Pork

Ingredients

1 kg/ 2-2 ½ lb pork – boneless joint with some fat around

To marinate:

2 dessertspoon honey
2 dtsp hoisin sauce
2 dtsp ground yellow bean sauce
4 dtsp light soy sauce
4 dtsp sugar
1 dtsp shaohsing wine or medium dry sherry
1 tsp salt

Method

1. Mix the above ingredients to marinate in a large bowl, place the pork in the marinade and allow to rest for 4-6 hours or leave it in the fridge overnight, turning occasionally.
2. Place the pork on a wire rack and roast in a preheated oven at Gas Mark 5 / 190C / 375F for 20 – 25 minutes
3. Remove from the oven, brush with the marinade and return to the oven with the bottom side up. Reduce the heat to Gas Mark 4/ 180C/ 350F and continue to roast for about one hour or until well done, then immediately brush all over with honey and return back to the oven for 3-5 minutes.
4. Cut into slices and serve hot with rice or noodles.

Sorpatel is a national dish of Goa, cooked on special occasions. It tastes better as it matures. Every recipe is different according to the individual's taste. It should be cooked at least three days in advance and should be heated once a day to bring out its taste. It goes well with pullau and sanna.

Ingredients

1½ kg/ 3lb 3 oz pork belly
½ lb lean pork
½ lb liver
½ lb heart
½ lb kidneys
3 large onions
20 Kahsmiri chillies, de-seeded
1 teaspoon cumin seeds
10 peppercorns
12 cloves
1½ teaspoons turmeric powder
6 green cardamoms, powdered
1 pod of garlic
1½" piece ginger
2 x 2" pieces of cinnamon
2 tbsp feni (optional)
3 tablespoons oil
vinegar and salt to taste

Method

1. Cut the pork into large pieces. Boil it with enough water to cover the meat and cook for 30 minutes. Spoon out the meat and leave aside to cool.

2. In the remaining stock add the liver, heart, kidneys and boil for approximately same time limit. Add water if required. Reserve any stock that is left over.

3. Grind all the spices in vinegar to a smooth mixture.

4. Cut the pork and other ingredients into small dainty cubes.

5. Heat some oil in a pan and fry the pork fatty pieces, then lean pieces. Lastly fry the liver, heart, and kidney in the remaining oil.

6. Heat the remaining oil in a large pan. Fry the onions till brown. Add the fried meat to the pan.

7. Then add the ground masala and stir well to coat the meat. Add the reserved liquid. Simmer on very low heat for at least one and half-hour, stir occasionally. Slow cooking is very important.

8. Add vinegar, salt and feni (optional). Cook for few minutes. Cool and leave aside for a day in the refrigerator.

9. On the next day, heat through on a low fire and bring it to boil. Adjust seasoning, if necessary.

10. Continue the process on the next day. The dish is now ready to be served.

My children are very fond of Goa sausages. Every year we bring some from Goa for the family. Making sausages and stuffing into sausage casings (guts) can be a tedious and time-consuming task. A lot of experience is required.

For the last two years I have been preparing the meat and storing in jars to last for three months. As a matter of fact, the taste of the home made sausage is irresistible and the quality of the meat is much superior. Instead of bringing sausages, I now bring a few bottles of Goa vinegar and make a batch to last for three to four months. It is very important to use a clean spoon whilst removing the meat for cooking.

Ingredients

2 kg leg of pork (lean)
1 kg belly
3 tablespoon salt
18 cloves
4 pods of cardamoms
18 peppercorns
1 ½ tsp cumin seeds

2 x 2" cinnamon stick
3 tablespoon of garlic paste
38 dried Kashmiri chillies
1 tablespoon of turmeric powder
2 tablespoon of ginger paste
4 cups of Goa vinegar

Method

1. Wash the meat and leave it to drain by hanging in a loincloth for couple of hours.

2. Cut the meat into small cubes. Mix in salt and place it in a large bowl. Cover it with a lid and place some weight and leave it for a day.

3. Spread a clean cloth on a board, then place the meat thinly on it to dry in the sun for half a day if the sun is strong.

4. Grind all the above spices in vinegar.

5. Place the meat in a large earthenware or glass jar. Add the spices and sprinkle on a little salt. Mix well. Add sufficient vinegar to cover the meat mixture.

6. Cover the mouth of the jar, so that the aroma of the meat remains intact. Cover the jar with thick double cloth. The mixture should be stirred every single day.

7. After three days the meat should be ready to be filled.

8. Wash the jars thoroughly and sterilise them in the oven.

9. Put the meat in the sterilised jars and cover it tightly, so that air does not get in.

Alternatively, stuff the sausage meat in casings (guts) and tie them in sections according to sizes. Place them in the sun to dry for up to three to five days.

Tandoori Pork steaks

Ingredients

4 x 150g (6 oz) pork steaks
150g natural yogurt
1 tbsp vegetable oil
2 tbsp lemon juice
Lemon wedges and fresh coriander to serve
1 red onion finely sliced
4 tbsp tandoori curry powder

Method

1. Mix the yogurt, tandoori curry powder, oil and lemon juice in a non-metallic bowl. Add the pork steaks and allow to coat in the marinade. Cover and leave to marinate for up to 2 hours.

2. Pre-heat the grill to medium. Place the pork steaks on a foil-lined grill pan. Grill for 6-7 minutes each side until cooked through and lightly charred in places.

3. Serve the chops with green salad, garnished with onion slices, lemon wedges, and fresh chopped coriander.

LAMB DISHES

Lamb with Dal Curry

This is a delicious and wholesome dish. Serve with chapattis or rice

Ingredients

½ cup masoor dal
1 onion chopped
1 medium size tomato
1 tablespoon of lemon juice
1 tsp of garlic and chilli paste
salt to taste
½ tsp mustard seeds
3 tomatoes chopped

1 lb lamb of shoulder cut into small pieces
½ tsp ginger paste
½ teaspoon cumin seeds
½ teaspoon mustard seeds
½ teaspoon turmeric powder
½ pint of water
1 tbsp chopped coriander

Method

1. Boil the dal with water and turmeric powder for about 10 minutes and leave aside.
2. Fry the onion and when golden brown add the garlic and ginger paste and tomatoes.
3. Simmer for a minute then add the lamb pieces and stir well.
4. Cover the saucepan and cook on very low heat for about 10 to 15 minutes, stirring occasionally.
5. Uncover the saucepan and add cooked dal and water. Cook until the sauce is thickened and the meat is soft.
6. Add the salt and lemon juice to the meat and simmer for a few minutes.
7. Fry separately the cumin and mustard seeds and add to the pan. Garnish with the chopped coriander.

Lamb or Mutton Xacuti

Xacuti is one of the traditional and delicious dishes of Goa. The same ingredients and same method can be used to make chicken and beef Xacuti. This dish tastes better when prepared one day in advance.

Ingredients

1 kg leg of lamb cut into one inch cubes
3 teaspoons coriander
10 Kashmiri red dried chillies (de-seeded)
½ teaspoon cumin seeds
1 teaspoon fenugreek seeds
5 peppercorns
2 tablespoon whole almonds peeled
150 grams grated or desiccated coconut
½ teaspoon turmeric powder
4 cardamoms peeled
6 cloves
¼ teaspoon cinnamon powder
1 tablespoon vegetable oil
1 small onion finely sliced
juice of one lemon or Goa vinegar
salt and sugar to taste
150 ml or 5 fl oz water

Method

1. Apply a little salt to the lamb pieces and set aside.
2. Roast the coriander, chillies, cumin, fenugreek, pepper, almonds, cloves, cardamoms and coconut in a dry pan. Grind all finely with water.
3. Add the turmeric and cinnamon powder.
4. Heat the oil and fry the onion until soft and slightly brown in colour then add the ground masala and fry for a few minutes.
5. Add the lamb pieces, water and mix well. Cook on a low heat for about 45 minutes, stirring occasionally. Add more water if necessary.
6. When almost cooked, add lemon juice, sugar and salt to taste.

Lamb Kidneys with Bacon

Ingredients

1lb / 450g lamb kidneys
4 rashers of bacon cut into small pieces
milled black pepper
6 mushrooms thinly sliced
1 medium green pepper sliced
1 small onion cut into slices
1 tomato cut into 4 pieces
2 tablespoons of white wine
1 tablespoon vegetable oil

Method

1. Cut the lamb kidneys into three pieces and sprinkle on the milled black pepper. Heat the oil in the frying pan and fry the onion until soft.

2. Add the kidneys to the pan and fry on a low heat both sides.

3. Then add the bacon pieces and continue frying.

4. Lastly, add the mushrooms, green pepper, tomato and white wine and cook for about 5 minutes.

Mutton or Lamb Korma - Mild mutton curry

This recipe is a delicious and mild, suitable for young children or those who cannot cope with hot spicy food. It can be substituted with chicken or beef. Serve with boiled rice

Ingredients

1 lb/500g mutton or lamb fillet cut into cubes
1 inch piece of fresh ginger, peeled and grated
1 clove of garlic crushed
1 tbsp of tomato puree
1 tsp of Spice no 2 (pg 24)
12 oz /360g double cream or fromage frais
1 medium size onion chopped
2 tbsp vegetable oil
1½ oz /37g ground almonds
salt to taste

Method

1. Apply a little salt to the mutton and place it in a shallow dish.

2. Blend the ginger, garlic, tomato puree and the spices to a smooth paste.

3. Mix 6oz of double cream and one tablespoon of chopped onion to the paste mixture.

4. Rub the mixture on to the lamb and leave it to rest for one hour.

5. Heat the oil in a pan and fry the remaining onion until golden brown.

6. Incorporate the meat, a little at a time and fry to seal the meat all over.

7. Stir in the remaining marinade, cover and cook for about 25 minutes.

8. Blend the remaining double cream with the ground almonds and stir into the mutton.

9. Cook the mutton on a low heat for 1- 1 ½ hour, stirring occasionally. Add half cup of water or more, as necessary.

Fried Lamb Chops / Steaks

Ingredients

6 lamb chops or steaks
1 egg lightly beaten
breadcrumbs
salt to taste
vegetable oil for shallow frying
50 gm / ½ cup plain flour

Spices for grinding :

4 cloves of garlic minced
2 green chillies
30gm / ½ cup coriander leaves
½ tsp ginger minced
1 tsp cumin seeds
salt to taste
22 ml / 1½ tbsp lemon juice
½ tsp peppercorns

Method

1. Tenderise the chops or steaks with a rolling pin or meat mallet.
2. Grind all the ingredients into a smooth paste. Apply the paste to the chops or steaks and marinate for about two hours.
3. Heat the oil in the frying pan. Roll the chops or steaks in the flour, and then dip in the beaten egg. Coat them with bread crumbs and fry for 5-7 minutes on each side till golden brown.
4. Serve hot, with green salad or boiled potatoes and peas.

Bev's Spaghetti Bolognaise Mince

This dish is delicious with pasta, lasagne, with ciabatta bread or even with rice.   My daughter Beverley prepares this dish often for her young boys.

Ingredients

500g/ 1lb steak mince or lamb mince
1 tsp of chopped fresh rosemary
1 tsp sweet basil
200 gm or 10 slices of streaky bacon chopped into small pieces
85g or 6 slices of Parma ham chopped
½ tsp freshly ground black pepper
3 cloves of garlic crushed
1 large onion chopped finely
8 fluid ounces of red wine
400g chopped tomato tin
100g/ 2 tbsp of tomato puree (optional sun dried tomato puree)
2 tbsp of olive oil

Method

1. Fry the rosemary with olive oil for a minute.
2. Add the bacon and Parma ham and fry for three minutes, then add the mince and cook for a further 3-4 minutes.
3. Add the onions and garlic and fry until the onions are soft and slightly browned.
4. Add the wine and cook for approximately 5 minutes or until the liquid is reduced to half.
5. Add the tomatoes, tomato puree, pepper and cook for 3 –4 minutes.
6. Place the cooked mince in the Pyrex or oven-proof dish, then bake for 1½ hours at Gas mark 4/ 350C /180F.
7. When ready garnish with sweet basil and serve with parmesan cheese.

Rogan Josh

Ingredients

1 kg/ 2.2 lb lamb fillet
1 cup natural yogurt
1 in piece of fresh root ginger, grated
1 tsp salt
½ tsp cumin seeds
2 cloves of garlic
3 tbsp lemon juice
4 tbsp oil

2 bay leaves
1 onion, finely chopped
½ pt/ 150ml water
4 green cardamom pods
1 tsp chilli powder
1 tbsp ground coriander
14 oz can of chopped tomatoes

Method

1. Trim away any excess fat from the meat, then cut it into one inch cubes.

2. Mix together in a bowl the lemon juice, yogurt, salt, one clove of crushed garlic and grated ginger.

3. Add the cubes of lamb and mix into the marinade until well coated. Marinate overnight in the fridge.

5. Heat the oil in to a large frying pan and fry the cumin seeds until they begin to splutter. Add the bay leaves and cardamom pods, then fry for about two minutes, stirring occasionally.

6. Add the onion and the remaining garlic and fry until onions are transparent. Stir in the ground coriander and chilli powder then fry briefly.

6. Add the marinated lamb and cook over a medium heat for five minutes, stirring occasionally.

7. Add the chopped tomatoes, tomato puree and water. Cover and simmer gently for about 1 - 1 ½ hours, or until the meat is soft and tender.

8. Serve with vegetable pillau rice or plain rice.

Chinese Paper-Thin Lamb with Spring Onions

This is a Chinese lamb recipe. It is slightly dry in appearance. It goes well with boiled potatoes and green salad.

Ingredients

½ lb lamb fillet, trimmed
2 cloves garlic, peeled and thinly sliced
2-3 bunches of spring onions, sliced into slivers
3-4 tbsp oil
Sesame oil 2-3 drops

Sauce :

½ tsp salt
½ tsp sugar
2 tsp dark soy sauce
2 tsp dry sherry or Shaohsing wine
1 tsp sesame oil

To marinate:

2 tsp thin soy sauce
2 tsp dry sherry or shaohsing wine

Method

1. Slice the meat thinly almost paper-thin slices. Put in a bowl.

2. Add the marinade ingredients and leave to marinate for 15-30 minutes.

3. Prepare the sauce by mixing all the sauce ingredients together in a small bowl.

4. Heat the wok until very hot. Add the oil and swirl it around. Add the garlic, let it sizzle and take on colour. Put in the lamb and turn and toss for 20-30 seconds or until partially cooked.

5. Pour in the sauce and add spring onions.

6. Continue stir-frying until the lamb is cooked and the mixture has absorbed most of the sauce.

7. Remove to a warm serving platter and sprinkle with sesame oil to enhance the flavour.

Bokri Tik Maas – Lamb in spicy red Gravy

This is a traditional Indian dish. The flavour is fantastic and I have used authentic Khasmiri whole chillies and other fresh spices. This dish can be served with boiled rice or chapattis.

Ingredients

1 kg lean lamb, cubed
4 fl oz (115ml) yoghurt
½ tsp of salt
½ lb onion, roughly chopped
1 tbsp chopped fresh coriander
2 inch fresh ginger
roughly chopped
2 cloves garlic
14 oz (400g) tin tomatoes
2 tbsp of margarine
3 tbsp of vegetable oil

Spice 1

3 green cardamons
3 cloves
1 inch piece of
cinnamon stick
½ tsp turmeric powder
4 Kashmiri dried chillies
1 tsp coriander seeds
1 teaspoon cumin seeds

Spice 2

1 tbsp garam masala
2 tsp paprika powder
a pinch of red food
colouring (optional)

Method

1. Put spice 1, except cardamoms, into a blender and blend into a smooth paste. Mix the lamb, yoghurt and salt. Leave it to stand for 6 hours or overnight.

2. Put the onion, ginger, garlic and tomato into blender, and puree.

3. Melt the margarine in a pan, add vegetable oil, and then add the onion puree. Cook for 10 minutes.

4. Put the lamb mixture into a separate pan (without any oil). Cook for about 20-30 minutes. Add salt to taste, and stir the meat occasionally to prevent sticking.

5. Combine the two mixtures and cook covered on a low heat for half an hour or so, until the meat is quite tender.

6. Add spice 2, and fresh coriander. Mix well and cook for a further 5 minutes, then serve.

7. If the curry gets too dry, a little warm water can be added. Alternatively, after both meat and puree have been fried, they can be put in a casserole dish in the preheated oven to Gas Mark 5 / 190C/ 175 F and baked for 45 minutes. Add spices 2 and cook for a further 10-15 minutes. Add fresh coriander and serve.

Goan Mutton Curry

This is a very popular dish in Goan households, especially for a Sunday meal. Serve with boiled rice.

Ingredients

1 lb mutton cut into small cubes
1 medium size onion cut finely
1 green chilli
1 tsp tamarind soaked in ½ cup of warm water
1 tbsp oil
salt to taste
2 tbsp yoghurt

Spices for grinding:

6 Kashmiri chillies
½ tsp cumin seeds
1 tsp coriander seeds
1 small onion
4 cloves of garlic
½ tsp turmeric powder
6 peppercorns

Method

1. Fry the onion and green chillies until soft.

2. Add the mutton pieces to the pan and cook for 5 minutes covered.

3. Uncover the pan and cook until all water has evaporated.

4. Add 1½ cup of boiling water and cook until the mutton is tender and all the liquid is absorbed. Alternatively, cook in the pressure cooker for about 10-15 minutes.

5. Grind the spices into a smooth paste.

6. Add the ground spices to the pan and simmer gently for 2 minutes until the meat is well coated with spices.

7. Add the tamarind juice and salt to taste. Stir and cook until the gravy is thickened and the meat is soft. Lastly, add the yoghurt and simmer on a low heat for 2-3 minutes.

Spiced lamb with legumes and vegetables. This recipe comes from the blend of two cultures: Parsees and Gujaratis from West India. It is very wholesome and my family's favourite dish. It is a very popular dish used in many parts of the world for its flavour. It also works well with chicken.　Serve with plain boiled rice.

Ingredients

100g/4oz (1/2 cup) toovar dal
1 medium onion sliced
25g/1oz (2 tablespoon) each
moong and masoor dal
1 tablespoon ground coriander
450g/1lb lamb or chicken meat
1 teaspoon ground cumin
175g/6oz mixed vegetables
for example aubergine, pumpkin, marrow
½ teaspoon chilli powder
fresh and frozen spinach
1 clove of garlic, crushed
½ tsp ginger paste
salt to taste
3 tablespoons tamarind juice
750ml / 3 ¼ cups water
½ teaspoon turmeric powder
2 tablespoons ghee

Method

1. Rinse thoroughly all the dal and then drain.　Cover with water and leave to soak for about 30 minutes.

2. Trim any fat off the meat and cut into small pieces.

3. Prepare the vegetables.　Remove the stalk from the aubergine and peel the pumpkin or marrow, then cut into cubes similar in size to the meat. Cut the spinach coarsely and set aside.

4. Drain the dals, place them in a pan with meat or poultry, vegetables, salt and water.　Bring to the boil, reduce the heat and cover the pan with a tight-fitting lid.

5. Simmer gently for 40-50 minutes or until the meat is tender and dals have been blended.

6. Remove from the heat and carefully lift out all the meat. Liquidize the dal mixture into a smooth puree. Return the puree and meat to the pan and allow to simmer gently while preparing the spice mixture.

7. In a separate pan heat the ghee. Add sliced onion and stir-fry to a rich golden brown in colour. Add all the spices and cook gently for a few minutes, stirring frequently to prevent the mixture from sticking to the pan.

8. Carefully pour the dal and meat mixture into the pan and stir to mix well.　Cover and cook the Dhan Sakh gently for 5 minutes until thoroughly heated.

9. Add the tamarind juice, stir vigorously and heat for 2-3 minutes.

BEEF DISHES

Beef or Mutton Assada

Ingredients

1 ½ kg / 3lb 3oz beef or mutton
4 green chillies
1 inch piece ginger
1 pod of garlic
2 teaspoon turmeric
½ teaspoon black pepper
3 onions sliced
2 tablespoon of vinegar and salt to taste
2 whole red dried chillies (cut into half and de-seeded)
2 tablespoon of oil

Method

1. Grind the chillies, ginger and garlic then add the turmeric and pepper powder.
2. Mix them all with vinegar to form a paste.
3. Tenderise the meat with a fork and rub in the mixture.
4. Marinate for about 6 hours or marinate overnight.
5. Heat the oil then add the onions and fry until golden brown.
6. Add the meat and brown evenly on all sides.
7. Incorporate the dried chillies and one cup of water.
8. Cover the pan and cook till tender

Green Masala Gravy

Ingredients

½ kg/ 500g beef (cubed)
1 inch piece ginger
10 cloves garlic
4 green chillies
3 onions finely sliced
1 teaspoon turmeric powder
½ teaspoon ground pepper
1 teaspoon sugar
2 tablespoon vinegar
salt to taste

Method

1. Apply the salt to the beef and set aside.
2. Brown the onions, add the meat and brown till the water dries.
3. Crush the ginger, garlic and green chillies.
4. Mix all the powdered masala and sugar with a little water to form a smooth paste.
5. Add the paste and the crushed ginger, garlic and green chillies to the pan.
6. Add warm water to cover the meat and cook till the meat is tender.
7. Lastly add the vinegar and cook a little more. (Adjust seasoning, if required.)

Mince Beef with Green Peas

This recipe applies for beef and mutton or lamb mince. Several other dishes can be prepared from this recipe, such as filling for samosas, potato chops and shepherd's pie.

Ingredients

½ kg /500g mince
3 large onions cut finely
½ tsp ginger paste
2 fl oz / 62ml water
1 tsp garlic paste
2 green chillies finely chopped
¼ teaspoon turmeric powder
½ teaspoon cayenne powder

1 teaspoon ground cumin
¼ teaspoon ground cinnamon
2 tomatoes finely chopped
bunch of coriander leaves
4 oz/ 120g frozen peas
2 tablespoon vegetable oil
2 tablespoon of vinegar or lemon juice
salt to taste

Method

1. Put the oil in a large pan and place it over a medium heat. When the oil is hot, add the onions, green chillies, garlic and ginger paste and stir. Fry until the onions are soft and slightly brown.

2. Add the remaining powered spices and stir for few seconds.

3. Add the tomatoes and cook on a medium heat until tomatoes have softened.

4. Add the minced beef and salt to taste. Cook and stir for couple of minutes, so that all the lumps are broken up.

5. Stir in the water and bring it to the boil. Simmer on a low heat for 15 minutes or until all the water is absorbed.

6. Add the vinegar and peas to the pan and return to simmer. Cover and cook on a low heat till the mince is almost dry.

7. Lastly add the chopped coriander and mix well.

Masachi Koddi - Goan Beef Curry

This is a popular dish in Goan households, an alternative to rice and fish curry. It is advisable to use rump steak. It is delicious and taste even better on the next day.

Ingredients

1lb /500g beef cut into cubes
1 medium onion chopped finely
½ coconut grated
2 tbsp vegetable oil
¼ coconut to extract milk
2 green chillies slit into half
6 Kashmiri chillies de-seeded

1 tbsp coriander
½ tsp cumin
1" piece turmeric
¼ tsp fenugreek seeds
300ml /1¼ cup warm water
salt to taste

Method

1. In a heavy frying pan roast the grated coconut on a low heat until lightly coloured. Set aside.

2. Then roast the rest of the ingredients until an aroma is emitted – it should take about 3 minutes.

3. Grind the roasted coconut and the spices with a little water.

4. In a saucepan sauté the onion until lightly brown. Add the meat and simmer for 10-15 minutes. When the liquid from the meat evaporates, add the ground spices and salt. Mix thoroughly.

5. Add the water and cook until the meat is tender. Add the coconut milk and cook for about 5 minutes. Serve with rice.

Bifes com Ovos – Fillet steak with egg garnish

This is an uncomplicated dish and easy to prepare. It is delicious to eat with fried potatoes or chips.

Ingredients

1 lb fillet steak cut into 4 slices weighing 4 ounces each
Salt and freshly ground pepper
1 tablespoon lemon juice
1 large clove of garlic crushed
1 tablespoon butter
2 large eggs lightly beaten
4 tablespoon of butter or oil
1 teaspoon of chives finely cut

Method

1. In a bowl mix together the salt, pepper and lemon juice.
2. Add the steaks, turning to coat with the mixture on both sides.
3. Leave it to stand for 15 minutes.
4. MIx the garlic with oil or butter melted.
5. In a frying pan heat the remaining oil or butter. Sauté the steaks over a moderate heat for 2 minutes, and then dip into the garlic butter.
6. Sauté for 1 minute longer, turn and repeat for rare steaks – cook a little longer for well done.
7. Transfer to a warmed dish and keep warm.
8. Mix the reserve marinade and chives with the eggs.
9. Add any remaining garlic butter to the pan and scramble the eggs, adding a little salt, if necessary, until they are just set and still soft.
10. Pile the eggs on to the steaks and serve immediately.

Bifes de cebolada – Fillet steak with onions

This is another simple steak dish served in Goa during Portuguese days. It goes well with green salad, onions and fresh tomatoes. Serve with mashed or boiled potatoes, sprinkled with coriander. A full-bodied dry red wine should go very well.

Ingredients

2 tablespoon butter
3 fillet steaks weighing 4 ounces each
salt and freshly ground pepper
2 large onions very finely sliced
4 tablespoon vegetable or olive oil
2 cloves of garlic chopped finely
2 medium tomatoes, peeled and chopped
1 tablespoon chopped coriander

Method

1. Heat the oil in a frying pan and sauté the onions over a moderate heat until soft.
2. Add the garlic and sauté for about 2 minutes. Add the tomatoes, season with salt and pepper and simmer until the mixture is thick and well blended, for about 10 minutes.
3. Stir in the coriander and cook for a minute longer. Set aside the sauce and keep warm.
4. Take another frying pan and heat the oil and butter.
5. Season the steaks with salt and pepper and sauté over a moderate heat for about 5 minutes on each side, if you want well done, and for medium rare about 4 minutes each side.
6. Lift out on to a warmed dish, pour the sauce over the steaks and serve with mashed or boiled potatoes, sprinkled with coriander.

Beef Rolls (Goan style)

Ingredient No. 1

1 lb frying steak, cut into six slices
3 slices of bacon, cut each slice into half
1 small potato peeled and cut into six slices
½ green pepper cut into slices
1 small onion sliced
freshly ground pepper
4 ounces of warm water

Ingredient No. 2

2 dried red chillies
½ inch ginger
4 cloves of garlic
1 medium onion
½ teaspoon turmeric powder
½ " cumin seeds
4 cloves
1 inch stick of cinnamon
2 cardamoms
2 tablespoons of Goa vinegar or wine vinegar
1 cup of water

Method

1. Tenderise the meat, so that the slices are spread thinly. Sprinkle with freshly milled pepper.
2. Place the tenderised steaks on the board and place on each a slice of bacon, potato, onion and green pepper.
3. Roll the steak to cover the fillings. Press it hard to form a beef roll. Tie the roll with a piece of thread.
4. Place the beef rolls in the frying pan and cover the rolls with a flat lid. On the lid place a pan with water for weight, so that the beef rolls are firm and pressed down.
5. Simmer on a moderate heat for about 20 minutes, open the lid and cook till all the liquid is absorbed. The beef rolls will remain firm.
6. Then add 4 ounces of water and cook for ten minutes.
7. Grind all the spices into a smooth paste.
8. Fry the onions, add the masala and fry.
9. Add one cup of water and bring it to the boil, then add beef rolls and cook until the gravy is reduced to half for about 20 minutes. Add vinegar and simmer for a minute longer.

Salt Meat

Ingredients

3lbs / 1½ kg joint of beef
2 tbsp salt
1½ tbsp saltpetre
4 fl oz vinegar
3fl oz lemon juice
½ tsp freshly ground black pepper

Method

1. Prick the joint with the fork and rub in the salt.
2. Roast the saltpetre and grind, and then add the vinegar and lemon juice.
3. Pour over the meat.
4. Put the meat in an earthenware or Pyrex dish. Cover the meat with a lid and keep under a weight in a cool place or refrigerator.
5. Prick and turn the meat twice a day for a week. If necessary, add little salt
6. Boil it with enough water to just cover the meat. Cook till tender.

Goan Beef Chilly Fry

Ingredients

1 lb meat
4 large onions
1 tsp of garlic and ginger paste (pg 29)
3 green chillies cut finely
6 peppercorns
½ inch cinnamon
½ tsp cumin seeds
1 tsp of tamarind soaked in 8 fluid ounces of warm water
1 large tomato chopped finely
1 medium potato chopped into small cubes
½ tsp of salt
½ tsp sugar
2 tbsp vegetable oil

Method

1. Grind the peppercorns, cinnamon and cumin into a smooth paste.

2. Cut the meat into small cubes and apply salt and ground paste.

3. Fry the onions until light brown, and then add the garlic and ginger paste, tomato, green chillies and the meat.

4. Cover the saucepan and cook for 20 minutes, stirring occasionally.

5. Uncover the saucepan and simmer until all the liquid has evaporated.

6. Add the tamarind juice and potatoes and simmer until the potatoes are cooked well. Adjust seasoning by adding salt and sugar.

Salt Tongue

Ingredients

1 tongue weighing 2 ½ to 3 lbs
2 tablespoon salt
3 tablespoon saltpetre
4 fl oz cup vinegar
1 tsp lemon juice
2 heaped tablespoon jaggery
½ tsp freshly ground black pepper

Method

1. Make a mixture of the salt, saltpetre.

2. Prick the tongue and rub the mixture on it.

3. Heat the vinegar and the lemon juice and dissolve the jaggery in it.

4. Pour over the tongue and keep in the refrigerator in an earthenware crock for 5 days turning it as often as possible.

5. Boil it with its juices, add water if necessary and cook till tender.

Ingredients

1 lb / ½ kg minced beef
4 rashers bacon
3 green chillies
2 slices bread (soaked and drained)
2 eggs
salt, pepper and nutmeg to taste

Method

1. Mince the bacon and green chillies.

2. Add the bread, eggs, beef and seasoning.

3. Shape into a loaf and place it in rectangular bread tin.

4. Alternatively, tie the loaf in a muslin cloth or grease-proof paper and steam in a vessel of boiling water for an hour.

Fried Calf Liver with Bacon

Ingredients

1 lb or 500g liver
4 flakes garlic cut into thin slices
4 fl oz water
6 rashers of bacon cut into small pieces
1 inch piece ginger chopped finely
3 green chillies
6 peppercorns
¼ teaspoon cumin
1 tablespoon of vinegar
salt and sugar to taste
4 onions chopped
2 tomatoes skinned and chopped

Method

1. Boil the liver with a little water, garlic and ginger for about five minutes. Reserve the stock.

2. Grind the green chillies, peppercorns and cumin.

3. Mix the ground spices with sugar, salt and a little vinegar.

4. Slice the boiled liver and apply the ground mixture, then set aside for half an hour.

5. Fry the bacon for three minutes, and then add the onions and when they turn golden brown add the tomatoes, the stock and the liver. Simmer on a low heat for 3-4 minutes or until the gravy is thickened. Serve with fried potatoes and green salad.

Masala Rump Steak

Ingredients

1 kg / 2lb 2oz rump steak
cut into ¼ inch thick slices
2 green chillies
1 inch ginger
4 cloves of garlic
salt to taste
½ teaspoon pepper
2 tablespoon vinegar
2 tablespoon soy sauce
2 tablespoon oil
2 medium size onions cut into rings
2 large tomatoes cut into round slices
2 tablespoons of water
2 tbsp of chopped coriander

Method

1. Tenderise each slice, apply a little salt, pepper and set aside.
2. Grind the chillies, garlic and ginger with vinegar and add the soy sauce.
3. Apply the ground masala to the steak and marinate for approximately 4 hours.
4. Heat a little oil in the frying pan and fry the onions for 3 – 4 minutes.
5. Drain and set aside.
6. In the same frying pan fry the tomatoes lightly and set aside.
7. Now fry the steaks on a very high flame, as many as the frying pan can hold. Turn and fry the other side.
8. When all the meat is cooked, mix the remaining marinade with water and pour into the frying pan and cook for five minutes. Reserve the gravy.
9. When all the steaks are done arrange them on a warm platter and garnish with onions, tomatoes and chopped coriander. Serve with boiled potatoes and gravy.

Beef Baffad

Ingredients

½ kg/ lb 2 oz beef cut into cubes
½ kg/ 1lb 2 oz mixed vegetables cut into cubes
8 fluid oz of water
½ tsp cumin seeds
4 Kashmiri chillies
1 tsp vegetable oil
½ tsp peppercorns
1 tsp coriander seeds
8 cloves of garlic
1 inch piece ginger
1 tsp turmeric powder
1 medium size onion finely chopped
2 green chillies chopped finely
½ tsp salt
2 tbsp vinegar

Method

1. Place the meat, vegetables and water in the saucepan and cook for 15 minutes and set aside.
2. Grind the cumin, chillies, pepper, coriander, 4 cloves of garlic, ½ inch ginger with two ounces of water, then add the turmeric powder and mix well.
3. Chop the onions, green chillies, remaining garlic and ginger finely.
4. Fry the onion in oil until golden brown, then add the chopped masala and fry for 30 seconds. Add the ground masala and fry for a minute.
5. Add the cooked meat, the vegetables and any left-over stock. Cover and cook on a slow heat till the meat is almost dry.

This is a Greek dish, very wholesome and nutritious. It is also a gluten free dish. Serve with boiled potatoes and green peas.

Ingredients

1 ½lb/ 700g aubergines cut into round slices
½ tsp salt
2 tbsp olive oil
1 large onion, finely chopped
1 kg minced lamb or beef
2 sprigs of thyme
1 tbsp finely chopped parsley
2 large tomatoes, skinned
2 tbsp tomato puree
4 tbsp dry white wine
freshly ground white pepper
2 tablespoon tomato puree
4 oz feta cheese crumbled (optional)

The sauce:

3 fl oz / 100 ml milk
3 fl oz/ 100ml double cream
1 egg
3 egg yolks

Method

1. Put the sliced aubergines into a colander, sprinkle with salt and leave to drain over a plate for 30 minutes.
2. Rinse the aubergines and pat dry with kitchen paper.
3. Heat the oil in a large frying pan and fry the onion until softened and lightly coloured.
4. Add the minced meat and fry, stirring often, until the meat has lost all its pinkness.
5. Add the herbs, tomatoes, tomato puree and white wine and cook gently, stirring from time to time, for 15 minutes. Season well with salt and pepper.
6. Make layers of the meat mixture then the layer of sliced aubergines in a large ovenproof dish, ending with a layer of aubergines.
7. In a small bowl, beat together the sauce ingredients and pour over the moussaka. Bake in the oven for about 50 minutes, to Gas mark 4 /180C/350F or until the top is crusty.
8. Heat the grill to high. Sprinkle the moussaka with the feta cheese and grill for 5 minutes, or until the cheese is melting and golden-brown.

Goan Red Beef Curry with Peanut Sauce

This dish is delicious and goes well with pillau rice or boiled potatoes and steamed vegetables to soak up the gravy.

Ingredients

1 small onion finely sliced
900g/2 lb rump steak, cut into one inch cubes
1 tbsp vegetable oil
6 oz/170g roasted ground peanuts
3 red chillies, seeded and sliced
5 tbsp red curry paste (see page30)
4 tbsp fish sauce

1 tsp sugar
1 pint/560ml coconut milk
3 lemon grass stalks, bruised
1 ½ tsp grated rind of green lime
Salt and freshly ground black pepper
Coriander leaves to garnish

Method

1. Fry the onion in a heavy saucepan until transparent. Add the red curry paste to the saucepan and cook for five minutes until fragrant comes through,. then add half of the coconut milk and heat, stirring, until it boils .
2. Add the fish sauce, sugar and lemon grass.
3. Continue to cook until the colour deepens. Add the rest of the coconut milk and stir to combine the flavour. Bring the mixture back to the boil.
4. Add the beef and the ground peanuts. Stir and leave to cook for 20- 25 minutes or until most of the liquid in the pan has evaporated.
5. Add the chillies and the grated rind of green lime. Adjust the seasoning to taste. Garnish with coriander leaves.

Ingredients

1 ½ lb lean stewing steak mince
1 large clove garlic finely chopped
1 egg yolk
½ cup chopped fresh coriander
oil for deep frying

Spice No. 1:

1 tsp coriander powder
½ tsp mango powder
1 tbsp cumin powder
1 dtsp gram flour

Spice No. 2:

1 tsp paprika
1 tsp turmeric
¼ tsp asafoetida
1 dessertspoon garam masala
1 tbsp dry fenugreek leaves

Sauce :

2 tablespoon margarine or corn oil
1 large onion, chopped
14oz (400g) tin tomatoes
8 fl oz water or stock

Method

1. Put the garlic, coriander, egg yolk and spices 1 through the blender and blend into a smooth paste.

2. Mix well with the mince, and then form into 1½ inch / 3-4 cm balls. You should get about 24 balls. Allow them to rest for 3 hours (or overnight) to dry out. Heat a deep-frying pan then add oil for deep -frying. Fry the balls for 2 minutes turning them regularly. Keep aside.

3. To make the sauce, heat the margarine and fry the onion. When golden brown, add spices 2. Mix and cook for a few seconds then add tomatoes. Add a little water and simmer for 10 minutes. Adjust the seasoning by adding salt to taste.

4. The sauce should not be thick nor too runny (thicken with rice flour or thin with water as required) Keep simmering, then add the meatballs. Simmer for a further 25 minutes, but avoid rigorous stirring, as you might break up the meatballs.

Lasagne

Ingredients

450 g (1 lb) lean minced beef
400 g (14 oz) can tomatoes
1 tbsp tomato puree
300 ml (½ pt) beef stock
salt and pepper to taste
12 sheets oven ready lasagne
50g (2 oz) Parmasan cheese, grated

Cheese Sauce:

75g (3 oz) butter
75 g (3 oz) plain flour
800 ml (1 ½ pt) milk
Pinch of grated nutmeg
50 g (2 oz) Cheddar cheese, grated

Method

1. Grease a 3 litre (5 pt) ovenproof dish.

2. Heat the oil in a large saucepan and fry the onions, garlic and carrots for 4-5 minutes. Add the mince and fry for 3-4 minutes or until brown. Stir in the tomatoes, tomato puree, stock and seasoning.

3. Simmer, covered, for 30 minutes or alternatively follow the recipe for Bev's spaghetti Bolognaise mince on page 95.

4. In a separate saucepan prepare cheese sauce by melting the butter, add the flour and stir for 1 minute. Remove from the heat and gradually add the cold milk. Bring it to the boil, stirring until thick, ensuring no lumps are formed. Season and add cheddar cheese. Or alternatively, follow the recipe for Bechamel Sauce on page 33.

5. Pre-heat the oven at Gas Mark 4 /180C /350F.

6. In the greased ovenproof dish, cover the dish with one-third of cheese sauce, then place over it four sheets of lasagne. Cover with half the meat sauce, then third of the cheese sauce.

7. Repeat layers, finishing with cheese sauce and sprinkle with Parmesan cheese.

8. Bake in a pre-heated oven for 45 minutes or until the lasagne is lightly browned.

Ingredients

½ kg / 500g beef cut into small cubes
170gm / 6oz pork cut into small cubes
110 gm /4oz Goa sausage cut into round slices
110gm /4oz carrot cut into small cubes
50gm /2oz green peas boiled
225gm /8oz potatoes cut into cubes
4 onions cut into fine slices
2 tomatoes cut finely
8 fl oz beef stock (beef stock cube can be used to make the stock)

Ingredients to grind:

3 green chillies
¼ tsp cumin
4 peppercorns
1 tsp of garlic and chilli paste
½ tsp turmeric powder
½ inch cinnamon stick
½ tsp ginger paste

Method

1. Grind all the ingredients together and apply to the meat. Allow to marinate for two hours.

2. Fry the onions until lightly browned, then add the tomatoes and meat.

3. Cover and cook until the liquid from the meat has been absorbed

4. Add the sausages and the beef stock. Simmer for 10 minutes.

5. Add the vegetables and cook on a low heat until all the vegetables are well cooked.

Beef with Black Bean Sauce

This is my family's favourite Chinese dish. This recipe is quick and easy to prepare and yet extremely flavoursome. Serve with fried rice or boiled rice and stir fried vegetables.

Ingredients

1 lb/ 500g rump steak
1 large carrot cut into long thin slices
1 green pepper de-seeded and cut into round slices
2 tbsp black bean sauce
1 tbsp dark soy sauce
1 inch ginger cut into paper thin fine slices
1 tbsp hoi-sin sauce
1 tbsp vinegar
½ tsp black peppercorns
½ tsp sugar
1½ tbsp white flour
vegetable oil for deep-frying

Method

1. Cut the rump steak into long thin strips, apply the soy sauce and leave aside.

2. Crush the peppercorns with a pestle and mortar to a fairly coarse texture, then combine with the flour. Sprinkle over the meat and mix thoroughly, ensuring each strip of meat is evenly coated.

3. Heat the oil until very hot in a wok. Lower the heat and deep fry the meat strips in batches for about 2-3 minutes until they are tinged with dark brownish colour. Remove them from the wok with a slotted spoon. Complete the process until all the meat is complete.

4. Deep-fry the carrot and pepper for about a minute. They should not be over-cooked.

5. In a small bowl combine the remaining sauces, vinegar and sugar.

6. Allow the oil to cool a little, then pour away all, but 2 tablespoons of it.

7. Add the ginger to the pan and stir-fry over a medium heat for a minute.

8. Add the sauce and stir over the heat for a minute until just heated through.

9. Transfer the meat to a heated serving dish and pour the sauce over it. Garnish with fresh coriander sprigs.

Braised beef with wine sauce

Ingredients

1 kg rolled joint of beef
25 g butter
4 bacon rashers
2 small glasses Marsala wine
230 ml/ 7 fl oz of red wine
1 large onion
1 clove of garlic crushed
2 celery stalks
½ tsp of freshly ground pepper
1 bay leaf
1 carrot
1 inch whole cinnamon
1 sprig rosemary
250 ml /8 fl oz beef stock
1 tbsp brandy
8 cloves

Method

1. Chop the carrot, onion, celery, rosemary and bacon.

2. Melt the butter in the frying pan and fry the chopped ingredients together with garlic, bay leaf, cloves, pepper and cinnamon for a few minutes.

3. Remove the ingredients with the slotted spoon and leave aside.

4. In the same fat brown the beef joint on all sides, when ready take the meat out.

5. In the same frying pan put the fried ingredients back in and sprinkle with a little red wine whilst continuing to heat. Continue to reduce until all the red wine has finished. Then add the beef stock and stir.

6. Add the joint and cook for two hours over a medium heat, covering the pan.

7. Take out the meat and place it on a warm serving dish.

8. To prepare the sauce, sieve the juices, return to the pan and add the Marsala wine and brandy, continue to simmer on a low heat and stir until the sauce begins to thicken. Remove from the heat.

9. Carve the meat into thin slices and pour the sauce over them and serve with boiled sweet potatoes .

FISH DISHES

Prawn curry with Coconut Juice

This is a perfect Goan prawn curry served in Goa with local rice. It tastes better on the next day. The same recipe can be used with any other available fish, such as fillet of haddock, kingfish, swordfish or salmon, but lady-finders should be omitted.

Ingredients

1 lb or 500 kg tiger prawns with shells on.
½ fresh coconut grated
6 Kashmiri dried chillies
2 Kokum
½ tsp cumin seeds
1 tbsp whole coriander
½ tsp turmeric powder
6 cloves of garlic
3 mango solam (dried mango slices)
1 tbsp tamarind
1 large onion chopped
salt to taste
240ml or 8 oz water
12 whole lady-fingers (okra) optional
1 tbsp vegetable oil

Method

1. Grind the coconut very finely, then add chillies, cumin, coriander, garlic, turmeric and tamarind. Grind into a smooth paste.

2. Peel and de-vein the prawns. Apply the salt and leave it to rest.

3. Fry the onion till brown. Then add the ground masala and fry well.

4. Add the prawns, kokum and dried mango slices. Cover with water and mix thoroughly, then bring it to the boil. Add the lady-fingers (if desired) and cook until the curry is thickened.

5. Add salt to taste.

Fresh Sardines cooked in the pressure cooker

Ingredients

12 Sardines
1 small onion
3 cloves of garlic crushed into paste
2 dried red chillies
1 tablespoon of olive oil
1 tbsp tamarind soaked in warm water
salt to taste
freshly milled black pepper
180 ml /6 oz of warm water

Method

1. Clean and wash the sardines. Apply the salt and pepper and place it in the pressure cooker.

2. Cut the onion into slices.

3. Break the red chillies into half and remove the seeds.

4. Soak the tamarind in warm water and squeeze with your hand until all the pulp of the tamarind is thoroughly extracted.

5. Add all the ingredients to the pressure cooker. Cover the pressure cooker and cook until you can see the steam coming out from the top of the pressure cooker. Place the weight and cook for about 12 to 15 minutes. The sardines will be firm and deliciously juicy.

Caril de Peixe a Goa – Fish Curry Goan style

This is a very popular dish of Goans. It is simple to make and any available fish can be cooked this way. All restaurants in Goa have this recipe on their menu as 'Rice and fish Curry' with fried fish or prawns.

Ingredients

Spices :

6 dried red Kashmiri chillies
8 cloves of garlic
1 tbsp of coriander seeds
½ coconut grated
1 tsp turmeric powder
½ kg fish sliced
1 onion sliced finely
2 green chillies, slit into halves
1 tbsp tamarind soaked in 1 cup of warm water
2 dried mango solam (mango slices)
salt to taste

Method

1. Clean the fish, apply the salt and set aside.
2. Put the coconut, a little water and all the spices into a food processor and blend into a smooth paste.
3. Put the ground masala in a saucepan with 2 cups of water and add the sliced onion.
4. Bring it to the boil, reduce the heat and simmer for about 25 minutes.
5. Add the tamarind pulp and mango solam, keeping the liquid level same as before.
6. Add the fish, bring it to the boil, reduce the heat and simmer.
7. Add the slit green chillies for added pungency. Cook for 5 to 6 minutes.
8. Adjust the seasoning to taste and remove from the heat.

Lagosta de Pobre – Poor people's lobster

Monkfish has the firm texture of lobster and a flavour quite similar to the magnificent shellfish. Kingfish can be a substitute in Goa.

Ingredients

1 lb monkfish, boned and cut into 1½ inches slices
4 cloves of garlic crushed
salt and freshly ground pepper
½ teaspoon paprika
3 fl oz dry white wine
2 tablespoon olive oil
½ leek cut into fine rounds
½ red pepper cut into long strips

Method

1. Put the monkfish into a bowl. Mix together the garlic, 1 tablespoon of olive oil, salt, pepper and add to the fish. Mix well to coat all over.
2. Leave for 15 minutes for the flavour to blend.
3. Heat the remaining oil in a casserole and add the leek and red pepper. Stir-fry lightly then add the fish and seasonings to the casserole. Turn the pieces to coat in the oil. Pour over the wine and cover the casserole with lid.
4. Pre-heat the oven Gas Mark 6/200C/400F and cook in the oven for about 20-25 minutes.
5. Serve the fish with the pan juices, boiled potatoes and peas or green salad.

Ambot – Tik Curry – Hot and Sour Fish Curry

This is one of the favourite fish dish of my family. It has a unique taste and delicious with any coarse fish, such as skate, shark (rock salmon) catfish or tinned sardines.

Ingredients

½ kg fish
1 ½ tsp oil
1 medium onion, sliced
1 tbsp of tamarind soaked in 1 cup of warm water
3 dried kokum and 3 dried mango slices
salt to taste
Grind finely the following spices with a little water
7 dried red Kashmiri chillies
3 peppercorns
4 cloves of garlic
½ tsp turmeric powder
½ tsp cumin seeds
2 fl oz of water

Method

1. Wash and cut the fish as required and sprinkle on a little salt. Set aside.

2. Heat the oil in a pan and fry the onion till golden brown.

3. Add the ground masala, one cup of the tamarind pulp and a little water. Bring it to the boil and add the kokum, dried mango and salt. Simmer on a low heat for about 10 minutes.

4. Add the fish and lower the heat. Simmer till done.

5. Adjust the seasoning if desired.

6. Serve with plain boiled rice.

Peixe Recheados – Stuffed Fried Fish

This dish is very common in Goa, especially stuffed mackerel, mullet, kingfish or pomfret, but any fish can be cooked this way.   Instead of rechear masala you can substitute with green chilli and coriander paste. See Page No.28. Serve with green salad or with rice and curry as an accompaniment.

Ingredients

3-4 small mackerel or 1 large pomfret
½ tsp salt
2 tbsp rechear masala (recipe on page 30)
oil for shallow frying

Method

1. Clean and wash the fish well. Make a slit along both sides of backbone almost across the fish, but do not separate the fish.

2. Apply salt and set aside.

3. Fill with rechear masala inside the slits, and tie together with a piece of thread.

4. Keep aside to marinate for an hour or two.

5. Heat the oil in a frying pan and shallow fry the fish over a medium heat, turning it to achieve a deep brown colour.

Caril de Caranguejos - Crab curry

Crab curry is delicious, but the cleaning of the crab can be tedious.

Ingredients

6 medium sized crabs about 1 kg in weight
2 inch piece ginger, finely ground
4 cloves garlic finely ground.
1 tbsp chilli powder
1 tsp cumin powder
2 tbsp oil
3 medium onions, sliced
1 tsp tamarind soaked in one cup of water.
Salt to taste

Method

1. Wash the crabs well in several changes of water and plunge them into the boiling water.
2. Cook till they turn red. Lift them out of the pan and cool. Break off the claws and legs, separate the shell from the body, and remove the apron and feathery gills from the underside. Remove the stomach from between eyes. Cut the body in half.
3. Mix the ginger, garlic and powdered spices with a little water to make paste.
4. Heat the oil in a pan and fry the onions till soft. Add the spice paste and fry for 2 minutes, adding a little water to prevent sticking.
5. Add the tamarind pulp, salt and crabs. Stir and mix well.
6. Add 4 fl ounces of water, reduce the heat and simmer for about 15 minutes, till done. Adjust the seasoning to taste and serve.

Caldinho de Peixe - Mild Fish curry

This dish is mild enough for children to enjoy. It tastes better with any white fish, such as mullet, mackerel, any filleted fish and lady fish. It can be served with rice, boiled potatoes or bread to soak up the gravy.

Ingredients

For curry masala:

1 coconut grated
½ tsp ginger paste
1 tsp coriander seeds
8 peppercorns
2 green chillies, de-seeded
8 cloves garlic
½ tsp turmeric powder
1 tsp rice flour
2 fl oz of water

Caldinho masala:

1 tbsp oil
1 medium onion, sliced
pulp of 1 tsp tamarind soaked in ½ cup of warm water
3 cloves, powdered
½ piece cinnamon, powdered
1 lb fish, sliced and lightly salted
salt to taste

Method

1. Put all the ingredients for curry masala and the water into a food processor and blend coarsely.
2. Squeeze the paste by hand over a strainer, to extract thick milk.
3. Add one cup of hot water to the paste, mix well and squeeze again to extract thin milk in a separate container.
4. Heat the oil in a pan and fry the onion till golden brown.
5. Pour in the thin milk from the curry masala and simmer. Add the tamarind pulp and powdered spices. Cook for 6 minutes. Add the fish and simmer till done, for approximately 3-4 minutes.
6. Add the thick milk, salt to taste and simmer for a few minutes. Adjust the seasoning.

Butterfly King Prawns

King prawns are plentiful in Goa and they are very reasonable in price. This is a delicious Chinese dish.
Serve on a bed of lettuce leaves or crispy green salad.

Ingredients

450 gm / 1 lb uncooked headless king prawns in their shells.
1 tsp fresh ground black pepper
1 tbsp light soy sauce
1 tbsp corn flour
1 tbsp Chinese rice wine or dry sherry
2 eggs lightly beaten
4-5 tbsp breadcrumbs
3 spring onions to garnish

Method

1. Peel the prawns, but leave the tails on. Split the prawns in half about three-quarters of the way through leaving the tails still firmly attached.

2. In a bowl prepare the marinade by using soy sauce, pepper, wine and cornflour. Add the prawns and leave them to marinate for about 10-15 minutes.

3. Dip the prawns one at a time in the egg mixture, and then roll the egg-covered prawns in breadcrumbs.

4. Heat the oil in the wok until medium hot. Gently lower the prawns into the oil by holding the tails. Deep-fry the prawns in batches until golden brown. Remove with a slotted spoon and drain on the kitchen paper. Garnish with spring onions.

Salmon steaks with Hollandaise sauce

This is also my husband's favourite dish. It is simple and easy to cook and can be cooked with any other filleted fish, such as monkfish, haddock, tuna and kingfish.

Ingredients

½ kg salmon steaks, de-boned and cut into six slices
1 tbsp olive oil
2 fl oz of water
2 fl oz of milk
freshly ground pepper
½ tsp lemon juice
1 tbsp parsley chopped coarsely

Method

1. Boil the salmon with water, milk, salt, freshly ground pepper and olive oil for five minutes.

2. Leave it to cool.

3. Gently lift the salmon and peel the skin off the salmon.

4. In a separate bowl prepare the hollandaise sauce shown on Page 31.

5. Place the salmon steaks in a serving dish and pour the hollandaise sauce over them. Garnish with chopped parsley.

83

Mixed Fish Casserole

This dish can be served hot during winter days and cold during summer with a green salad.

Ingredients

6 medium sized onions, finely chopped
2 fl oz/ ¼ cup olive oil
3 medium sized garlic cloves, crushed
1 large green and red pepper, white pith removed, seeded and cut into strips
1 tbsp chopped fresh basil or 1 ½ tsp dried basil
1 lb tomato blanched and peeled and sliced
¼ tsp chilli powder
¼ tsp ground cumin
8 oz halibut steaks or king fish steaks
2 medium sized mackerel fillets, skinned
8 oz cod steaks, skinned
½ tsp salt
¼ tsp freshly ground black pepper
1 tbsp white wine vinegar

Method

1. In a small saucepan heat the oil over moderate heat. When the oil is hot, add the onions and garlic and cook, stirring occasionally, for about 5 to 6 minutes, or until the onions are soft and translucent but not brown.

2. Add the peppers, basil, tomatoes, chilli powder and cumin. Cover the saucepan, reduce the heat to low and simmer for 1½ hours, or until it resembles a thick sauce.

3. Transfer the sauce to a large casserole dish and add the fish, salt and pepper and stir well to mix.

4. Preheat the oven to Gas Mark 3/ 170C/325F. Place the casserole in the oven and bake for 25 to 30 minutes or until the fish flakes easily when tested with a fork. Remove the casserole from the oven and stir in the vinegar. Serve immediately with boiled potatoes and green vegetable.

Paper Wrapped Fish

This recipe can be served with chilly sauce on page 33. It goes well with boiled potatoes and green salad.

Ingredients

To marinate:

1 lb cod or haddock
½ tsp salt
1½ tablespoon light soy sauce
3 tbsp dry sherry wine

1 tsp cornflour
1 ½ tbsp oil
1 tsp sesame oil

For filling :

2 inch ginger root – sliced very thinly
3 spring onions cut into 2 inches long
oil for deep frying
Wax paper or grease-proof paper cut into 8"x 8". Brush each piece with oil

Method

1. Clean the fish and drain it on the kitchen paper. Slice each piece to a thick size of 6"x 2".

2. Marinate the fish with the above ingredients. Mix thoroughly and leave it to marinate for 10-15 minutes.

3. Place 1 or 2 pieces of fish on each paper with 1-2 slices of ginger on one side and spring onion on the other side. Fold into envelopes.

4. Put the oil in a wok or a heavy pan for deep-frying. Bring the oil to the boil on high heat. Lower the heat to medium.

5. Deep-fry and unwrap the fish then place them on the kitchen paper.

6. Arrange on a warm plate and serve hot.

7. Pour the used oil into a container for later use.

This is a Chinese recipe. Any white fleshy fish is suitable, such as cod, haddock, mullet and King-fish or any other firm white fish. This is also a gluten free dish.

Ingredients

½ lb fillet of cod or haddock or small grey mullet
1 small egg beaten
2-3 dessertspoon(dtsp) corn flour
cooking oil for deep-frying

Mixture A:

[1"fresh ginger root, peel it lightly and squeeze the juice with garlic press
[1 tsp shaohsing wine or medium dry sherry
[1 teaspoon salt

Sauce:

Mixture B:

[4 dtsp wine-vinegar
[4 dtsp sugar
[4 dtsp tomato ketchup
[1 tsp salt
[1 dtsp shaohsing wine or medium dry sherry
[¼ pt or 5 fl oz water

1 teaspoon cornflour dissolved in 1 dtsp water (cornflour paste)
3 dtsp cooking oil
1-2 clove garlic crushed & chopped
1 small shallot sliced thinly
1 small tomato – cut into 6 slices
2-3 dtsp small green peas cooked
1-2 slices of pineapple (optional) cut into small cubes
1 inch fresh ginger root –cut into fine threads

Method

1. Prepare the fish as a fillet or leave as a whole fish. Wash and pat dry.

2. Marinate with Mixture 'A'. Keep aside.

3. Prepare mixture 'B' in a bowl.

4. Prepare the corn flour paste.

5. Prepare all ingredients and arrange them in separate plates.

6. Heat the wok and add the oil for deep-frying. While the oil is heating, coat the fish with beaten egg on both sides then sift the corn flour over. When the oil is boiling hot, deep fry the fish. Remove it to a serving dish and keep warm.

7. Clean the wok and reheat it and add 2 dessertspoon of oil. Bring it to the boil then add the sliced shallot and ginger. Stir for few seconds, mix in garlic, stir until it changes colour to light golden.

8. Add in the tomato, pineapple and green peas. Stir well.

9. Mix in sauce 'B' and stir again. Continue to boil, stir in the corn flour paste to thicken the sauce. The sauce should not be too thick.

10. Finally stir in 1 dessertspoon of oil and pour the sauce all over the fish.

11. Serve hot with boiled rice.

Fish Pie with cheese topping

Any white fillet fish is suitable for this dish, such as cod, halibut, and haddock or even salmon. This dish is perfect for entertaining as it can be made well in advance and re-heated in the oven just before you serve the dinner. It can be prepared as a gluten free pie, by substituting corn flour and rice flour, instead of wheat flour.

Ingredients

½ kg / 1 lb of haddock (filleted)
1 large carrot finely sliced into rounds
2 leaks cut into rounds
1 small pepper diced
2 large florets of cauliflower
100gm of cabbage diced
salt and freshly ground pepper
8 new potatoes boiled and sliced thinly
1 tbsp parsley cut coarsely
8 fl oz of water

White sauce:

113gm/4oz grated cheese
2 tbsp corn flour
1 tbsp plain flour or rice flour
28gm/ 1oz ghee or margarine
6 fl oz fish and vegetable stock
2 fl oz of milk

Method

1 Wash the fish, apply the salt and freshly ground pepper. Boil it with 4 fluid ounces of water. Cool and flake the fish, discarding skin and any bones. Reserve the fish stock
2 Boil the vegetables with the remaining water and a little salt. Again reserve the stock.
3 Place the vegetables in a large oven-proof dish as the first layer
4 Spread the fish flakes over the vegetables and then place the sliced potatoes to cover the fish.
5 Sprinkle with freshly ground pepper and parsley.
6 Prepare a white sauce by using the given ingredients. Melt the butter in a saucepan. Remove the saucepan from the heat, stir in the corn flour and plain flour, then cook gently over a low heat for a couple of minutes, stirring constantly until the flour is well cooked. Add the fish and vegetable stock and milk a little at a time, stirring vigorously. When the sauce begins to thicken and starts bubbling, remove from the heat and stir in half the quantity of the cheese.
7 Pour the white sauce over the potatoes and sprinkle with the remaining grated cheese.
8 Preheat the oven Gas Mark 4 180C/350F and bake the pie for 45 minutes to 1 hour or until its colour is changed to golden brown.

Mackerel Kebabs

Mackerels are plentiful and reasonably cheap in Goa. This dish is delicious and attractive if served on a bed of green salad, sliced red tomatoes and garnished with sliced lemon.

Ingredients

6 Mackerels, cleaned, gutted and with their backbones removed
9 small pickling onions
9 cherry tomatoes
9 button mushrooms, wiped clean and cut into halves
2 medium sized green peppers, white pith removed,
seeded and cut each pepper into six strips.
3 fl oz (3 tbsp) white vinegar
4 fl oz (4 tbsp) olive oil
¼ tsp black pepper
¼ tsp salt
1 tsp dried oregano

Method

1. Cut each mackerel into 4-6 slices depending on the size of the mackerels.
2. In a large shallow dish, combine the oil, vinegar, salt, pepper and oregano.
3. Thread the slices of mackerel on to skewers alternating with the tomatoes, mushrooms, onions and green pepper strips.
4. Place the prepared skewers in the shallow dish to marinade for about 2 hours at room temperature, turning occasionally.
5. Remove the kebabs from the marinade and place under the pre-heated grill and cook for 10-12 minutes, basting the kebabs with the marinade and turning them frequently, so that they are cooked evenly.
6. Taste the fish with a fork; when cooked the fish will flake easily

VEGETABLE DISHES

This is a favourite dish of my second son. It is simple and quick to prepare, yet delicious with tangy taste. It goes well with boiled rice or boiled potatoes and any other main meat dish.

Ingredients

4 medium size courgettes grated
1 medium onion peeled and cut into fine slices
1 teaspoon salt
½ tsp mustard
freshly ground pepper
½ tsp cumin
¼ tsp turmeric powder
1 green chilli
2 tbsp yoghurt
1 ½ tbsp vegetable oil
1 tbsp coriander powder
1 tbsp fresh coriander leaves chopped

Method

1. Apply a teaspoon of salt to the courgettes and leave to stand for half an hour.

2. In a saucepan fry the onion until light golden brown then add mustard seeds and fry briefly. Squeeze all the water from the courgettes by pressing the mixture with your hands. Then add the courgettes to the saucepan with cumin, turmeric, coriander and green chillies.

3. Stir well and simmer for about five minutes on a moderate heat.

4. Lastly put in the yoghurt and continue to simmer briefly. Garnish with coriander leaves.

Fried Rice with Egg and vegetables

This is a simple and wholesome dish to prepare. It can be served with any stir-fried meat or poultry.

Ingredients

2 pt level in a glass measuring jug
long grain cooked rice (refrigerated overnight)
1 large egg.
5 tbsp vegetable oil
3 medium size mushrooms cut into ¼ cm slices
2 oz Chinese cabbage finely sliced
1½ tsp light soy sauce
6 oz/ 160gm mung-bean sprouts washed and drained
2 oz / 60gm very finely sliced spring onions
½ red pepper diced into small pieces

Method

1. Heat 2 tbsp of oil in a wok over a medium heat. When hot, put in the mushrooms. Stir and fry for about 30 seconds. Remove the mushrooms with a slotted spoon and place them on a plate.

2. In the same oil stir and fry the Chinese cabbage and red pepper for 1 minute. Put them on the same plate with mushrooms. Sprinkle on ½ tsp of soy sauce.

3. Put the remaining oil into the wok and heat it at the same temperature. When hot, put in the rice and stir once. Make a hole in the centre of the rice and break an egg into the hole. Stir the egg, first in its hole and when it sets a bit, mix it up with the rice. Stir and fry the rice for a minute or two.

4. Now add the bean sprouts. Stir and fry for about 5 minutes. Add the spring onions, mushrooms, cabbage and pepper. Stir once and sprinkle the remaining soy sauce. Stir and fry for about 1 or two minutes. Serve immediately.

Sourak Curry

This is a very common Goan curry, prepared especially when the fish is scarce. It goes well with fish or pork parra, dried salt fish and pickles.

Ingredients

1 onion sliced thinly
½ grated coconut
1 teaspoon turmeric powder
1 teaspoon cumin seeds
4 cloves garlic
4 red dried chillies
salt to taste or a cube of vegetable stock
2 fl ounces of thick tamarind juice to taste
2½ cups of water
3 dried mango solam
2 kokum

Method

1. Rub the sliced onions with salt until they are soft and juicy.

2. Grind the coconut, cumin, garlic and chillies finely and put the mixture in a deep pan.

3. Mix the turmeric and onion with water then add the kokum and mango solam and boil for 15 minutes or until the liquid is reduced to half.

4. Add the tamarind juice, salt to taste and simmer the curry for further 10 minutes.

Egg Curry

Ingredients

8 hard boiled eggs cut into halves
½ grated coconut
1 onion finely sliced
1 medium tomato chopped
3 green chillies
1 teaspoon cumin
1 teaspoon of mustard seeds
4 cloves of garlic
½ teaspoon of turmeric powder
¼ inch piece of ginger
1 cup of tamarind juice
1 tbsp chopped coriander leaves

Method

1. Grind the coconut, chillies, cumin, mustard, garlic and ginger, then add the turmeric powder and mix well.

2. Fry the onion until light brown in colour. Add the tomato and fry until it is soft.

3. Add the masala and continue to fry for a minute.

4. Add the tamarind juice and bring it to the boil.

5. Cook for five minutes. Lower the heat and place the hard-boiled eggs gently In the gravy.

6. Cover the pan and cook on a low heat for a further 3 minutes.

7. Garnish with chopped coriander leaves.

Ingredients

2 medium size green mangoes weighing roughly ½ lb. Slice each mango into four slices.
1½ tablespoon coriander seeds
6 Khasmiri chillies
½ teaspoon cumin
4 cloves of garlic
½ inch piece ginger
2 onions sliced finely
1 tablespoon jaggery
salt to taste
4 cups of water

Method

1. Put the chillies, coriander, cumin, turmeric, garlic and ginger into a processor and blend into a smooth paste.
2. Fry the onions till golden brown.
3. Add the ground masala and fry well then add the mangoes and jaggery and cover with water.
4. Cook till the mangoes are soft and the curry is thick. Add salt to taste.

Mama's Scotch Eggs

During my heydays in Africa I was quite intrigued to watch the enthusiasm of my mother-in-law's cooking. She was a great cook and prepared delicious meals and snacks for the family.   Scotch eggs were one of the favourite dishes in her repertoire.

Ingredients

4 hard boiled eggs
½ kg potatoes
½ red pepper cut into small cubes
1 egg
2 spring onions finely chopped
1 teaspoon coriander chopped
1½ tbsp of egg mayonnaise
freshly ground pepper
breadcrumbs
salt to taste

Method

1. Boil the potatoes and cool them. Mash and set aside.
2. Cut the eggs lengthwise into halves.
3. Separate the yolks and place them in a bowl. Leave aside the outer coating of the egg in a separate dish.
4. Crumble the yolks, then add the other ingredients (egg mayonnaise, red pepper and spring onion) to the bowl and mix well.   Add pepper and salt to taste.
5. Divide the mashed potatoes into eight portions. Then take one portion and spread it in the palm of your left hand. Place the outer coating of the egg in the hollow part of the palm. Fill the yolk mixture and cover it with mash. Shape it in the form of an egg. Prepare all eight portions and place them in the dish.
6. Dip each scotch egg into the lightly beaten egg mixture, coat each one with breadcrumbs.
7. Heat the frying pan, then add the oil and bring it to the boiling point. Lower the heat to medium and fry the scotch eggs in shallow oil on both sides, turning occasionally until the colour changes to golden brown.

Sweet potatoes in batter

This is a simple and quick dish to prepare, yet it tastes delicious when eaten while hot. Serve with any dipping sauces.

Ingredients

1 lb/ 450 g sweet potatoes, peeled
¼ tsp salt
2 tbs plain white flour
vegetable oil for shallow frying
1 large egg

Method

1. Peel the sweet potatoes. Cut them crosswise resembling a diagonal shape with the thickness of ¼ inch or 1cm thick.

2. Spread the flour out on a plate. Dip the sweet potatoes slices in the flour so that they are well coated on all sides.

3. Break the egg in a shallow bowl, add the salt and beat the egg lightly.

4. Keep the frying pan on the heat and pour in some oil for shallow frying. Heat over a low medium heat until the oil is very hot.

5. Dip the sweet potato slice in the egg one at a time and place them in the frying pan, making sure that the slices lie in a single layer in the pan. Fry until the slices turn golden brown on one side. Turn them over and fry the second side to the same colour.

6. Remove the slices with a slotted spoon and drain on the kitchen paper. Serve immediately.

Egg Caldinho

Ingredients

3 medium size eggs
1 small onion finely cut
1 tbsp vegetable oil
3 cloves of garlic
½ inch ginger peeled
3 tbsp fresh grated coconut
6 peppercorns
½ tsp cumin seeds
1 tsp of coriander seeds
1 green chilli, slit into half
¼ tsp of turmeric powder
1 tsp of vinegar and salt to taste
2 fl oz of water

Method

1. Grind the garlic, ginger, peppercorns, cumin and coriander seeds into a smooth paste. Add the turmeric and mix well.

2. Grind the desiccated coconut with 4 ounces of warm water and extract the thick juice. Add another 4 ounces of warm water and remove the thin juice.

3. Pour oil in the heavy pan and when hot add the onion. Fry the onion until soft, add the masala paste and water then simmer for a minute.

4. Add the thin coconut juice and bring it to the boil. Lower the heat and simmer for five minutes.

5. Add the thick juice, vinegar, salt to taste and the green chilli. Bring it to the boil and simmer for a few minutes.

6. Break the eggs carefully one at a time, as not to break the yolks. Cover the pan and allow simmering on a low heat for about 10 to 12 minutes until the eggs are well cooked.

Masoor Dal with Green Spinach

This recipe can be cooked with different dals (mung dal, masoor dal or toor dal or combination of two dals in equal measures).

Ingredients

200g /1 cup masoor dal
1 teaspoon turmeric powder
3 medium size tomatoes chopped
250 grams spinach washed thoroughly and chopped
¼ inch piece of ginger
4 cloves of garlic
1 onion finely chopped
1 green chilli finely chopped
1 tsp cumin seeds
1 tsp mustard seeds
2 curry leaves
salt to taste

Method

1. Cook the dal with water and turmeric until soft.

2. Add the chopped tomatoes and cook till the tomatoes are pulpy.

3. Add the spinach to the dal, cook for 3 minutes, add the salt and set aside.

4. Grind the ginger and garlic into a fine paste.

5. In a separate frying pan fry the onion until golden brown, add the garlic and ginger paste and simmer for a minute, then add the green chilly, cumin, mustard seeds and curry leaves.

6. When the mustard seeds start to pop, pour the fried ingredients over the dal. Adjust the seasoning by adding more whatever you need.

Mergor of French Beans – French beans with coconut

Any green beans, cabbage, gourd, pumpkin or any other vegetable can be prepared in this way.

Ingredients

1 lb French beans cut into thin slices
1 large onion thinly sliced
1 tsp of spice No. 3 (page 25)
4 oz of water
1 large tomato skinned and chopped finely
1 tbsp vegetable oil
1 tbsp desiccated coconut
1 tsp of lemon juice
salt to taste

Method

1. Fry the onion until soft and transparent, then add the chopped tomato.

2. Mix the spice with a little water and add to the pan and simmer for a few seconds.

3. Add the French beans and the remaining water. Cover the pan and simmer on a low heat for 10 minutes.

4. Uncover the pan, and then add the desiccated coconut and lemon juice. Simmer until the sauce is thick and the vegetables are well done.

This is a South Indian speciality and served as a snack. There are several types of dosas. My favourite is masala dosa and it is prepared with potato bhaji fillings. Serve with the coriander chutney. (page 167)

Ingredients

2 oz black gram (Urid dhal)
1 tsp fenugreek seeds
10 oz /1¼ cup of rice flour
1 tbsp gram flour
salt to taste
vegetable oil or ghee for frying
½ tsp mustard seeds
1 tbsp chopped coriander leaves
4 cups of water

For filling:

½ lb potatoes boiled, peeled and cut into small cubes
½ lb onions cut into small pieces
2 or 3 green chillies
½ tsp turmeric
salt to taste
½ tsp mustard seeds

Method

1. Soak the black gram and fenugreek seeds for 2-3 hours.
2. Grind to a smooth paste with water and salt.
3. Mix the flour in to the batter. Add the water and mix thoroughly, so that you get smooth batter without any lumps.
4. Keep the batter overnight or for 8-10 hours to ferment.
5. Heat the heavy and large frying pan and grease lightly with oil or ghee.
6. Spread the batter evenly into a thin round pancake.
7. Fry both sides till golden in colour.
8. In a separate pan heat the oil, add the onions and green chillies. After 2 minutes, add the potatoes, salt and turmeric powder.   Mix well and simmer for another 2-4 minutes.
9. Place the prepared dosa on a serving plate, put 3 tablespoons of potato bhaji on half the dosa and fold over.   Serve hot with your preferred chutney.

Red Bhaji of Goa - Red Spinach

Red spinach is my favourite vegetable.   It tastes delicious when fresh and tender. Every year I bring the seeds from Goa and I grow them in my green-house in the summer.

Ingredients

2 large bunches of red spinach
1 large onion sliced
½ teaspoon of garlic
2 green chillies de-seeded and slit into half
2 tablespoon of olive oil
1 tablespoon of dried prawns or fresh prawns (optional)
1 large tomato
2 mango solam
salt to taste

Method

1. Wash the spinach thoroughly in several changes of water to remove any grit or mud. Drain it.
2 Heat the oil in a pan, add the onion and fry until soft, add the prawns, chopped tomato, garlic paste, mango solam and chillies. Fry for a minute.
3 Cut the spinach coarsely together with soft stock and add to the pan. Add two tablespoons of water, cover and cook over a low heat for about ten minutes. Stir frequently to prevent sticking.   Add salt to taste. It goes well with rice.

Matoke (Green Plantains)

Most bananas/plantains (savoury bananas) are grown in tropical regions from the Caribbean to Africa, India and Southeast Asia. When we lived in Uganda we ate matoke at least once a week. It is a staple meal of Ugandans and often served with peanut sauce where the food budget is limited. This recipe should be served as soon as it is ready because the plantains tend to harden quickly. Serve with roast chicken, peas and carrots.

Ingredients

3 green plantains
1 tablespoon of ghee or margarine
1 medium size onion sliced
1 large tomato sliced
1 tsp juice of lemon
1 green chilli
½ teaspoon turmeric
3 slices of bacon cut into small pieces.
freshly milled pepper
salt to taste

Method

1. Boil some water in a large saucepan, which can hold the bananas and cook them in their skins for approximately 20-25 minutes, until they are soft.

2. Take them out of the pan and let them cool a while.

3. Peel off the skins and cut the bananas into thick rounds.

4. Heat the ghee or margarine in a pan, add the bacon and fry until crisp, then add the onion and cook until it is soft. Now add the tomato, green chilli and turmeric.

5. Lastly add the bananas and water and simmer on a low heat for about 10 minutes stirring occasionally.

6. Adjust seasoning to taste. Serve immediately.

Cabbage with fresh coconut

This recipe is very simple to make and in Goa various vegetables are cooked this way.

Ingredients

½ lb cabbage, finely shredded
1 tbsp of oil
½ tsp of garlic paste (page 29)
1 onion sliced
1 green chilly de-seeded and cut into four pieces
1 tbsp of grated coconut
salt to taste

Method

1. Heat the oil in a pan and fry the onion, garlic and green chilli till the onion is soft.

2. Add the cabbage and salt. Cover and cook over a low heat for five minutes. Add a little water if required.

3. When nearly cooked stir in the coconut and serve immediately.

Verdura Misturada - Mixed vegetable stew

This dish can be served as a vegetable with roast meat, beef or lamb. It also can be a vegetarian main course with rice, boiled potatoes or even garlic bread. When served cold excess liquid should be strained and reserved for soup.

Ingredients

1 large aubergine cut into small pieces
1 large onion cut in slices
3 spring onions chopped
1 tsp of garlic paste
2 medium size courgettes cut into small pieces
1 large carrot cut into tin rounds
Red, and yellow peppers (one of each)
400g chopped tomato tin
2½ tbsp strong olive oil
Salt to taste
Freshly milled black pepper
4 oz French beans
2fl oz of water

Method

1. Place the aubergine in a bowl of salted water and let it rest for 10 minutes.

2. De-seed the peppers and cut like all the other vegetables into small pieces. Squeeze out the water from the aubergine and pat dry with kitchen paper.

3. Sauté the onion until transparent then add the garlic paste and all the other vegetables, including the aubergine, salt and pepper. Mix all the ingredients together and bring to the boil.

4. Cover and simmer on a low heat for about five minutes.

5. Add the chopped tomatoes, stir again and cover the pan and cook gently for 40-45 minutes, stirring occasionally. Adjust seasoning to taste.

Red Pumpkin Mergor

Ingredients

¼ kg pumpkin
1 tbsp oil
½ tsp cumin seeds
1 medium onion sliced
1 tsp garlic and ginger paste (page 29)
¼ tsp turmeric powder
1 medium tomato chopped
4 oz water
salt to taste
2 large dried red chillies de-seeded and broken into two pieces
fresh coriander leaves for garnish

Method

1. Peel the pumpkin and cut into one inch cubes.

2. Heat the oil in a pan, add the cumin seeds and fry till they start crackling. Sauté the onion until transparent then add the tomato, chillies, turmeric, garlic and ginger paste. Stir-fry for a minute, and then add the pumpkin, salt and water.

3. Bring it to the boil, cover the pan with the lid and simmer on a low heat for about 10 minutes.

I was quite intrigued to create a recipe when I received a bottle of goat cheese from Gozo, Malta as a holiday present. Hence the name is derived from it. This recipe is supremely good version of appetizer to serve. Any goat cheese can be substituted.

Ingredients

8 oz goat's cheese, rind removed
1 red pepper, de-seeded and finely cut
1 red onion cut into fine rounds
2 tbsp French tarragon
2 tbsp parsley
1 tbsp mint
8 oz mixed salad leaves, shredded
4 oz honey ham cut into long strips

For the dressing:

2 tbsp wine vinegar
½ tsp of Dijon mustard
4 tbsp olive oil
salt to taste

Method

1. To prepare the dressing, mix the vinegar and salt then stir in the mustard. Blend in the olive oil gradually and season with ground pepper. Set aside.

2. Place the salad leaves in a bowl. Add half of the salad dressing and toss to coat.

3. Cut the goat's cheese into four round slices and grill for about 1-2 minutes. Place the goat's cheese on top of the salad leaves then scatter the pepper, onion, ham and herbs. Drizzle with the remaining dressing and serve as a starter.

Jasmine's Masoor Dal

My friend Jasmine prepared this dish for our dinner party and my family liked it very much. This is a vegetarian dish and it is very simple and quick to prepare. Serve with boiled rice and green salad or raita.

Ingredients

½ cup masoor dal
2 cups water
2 green chillies
½ tsp ginger paste
a pinch of asafoetida powder
salt to taste
lime (optional)
½ tsp cumin seeds
¼ tsp mustard seeds
curry leaves (optional)

Method

1. Put the dal, green chillies, ginger and water in the pressure cooker and cook for about 10 minutes. The dal should be over- cooked.

2. Remove the dal from the pressure cooker and put it in a pan and simmer it on a low heat if there is too much liquid. If it is too thick than add a little water.

3. Add the salt and lime juice.

4. Heat the oil in a separate frying pan and add the cumin seeds, mustard and asafoetida and fry until the mustard seeds start crackling. Pour the mixture over the dal and serve immediately.

Small aubergines should be used for this recipe. They can be baked or cooked on very low heat.

Ingredients

½ kg small aubergines
2 tbsp of oil
2 large onions cut finely
2 medium tomatoes finely chopped
2 green chillies
1 tsp of vinegar
1 tbsp of rechear masala on page 31
1 tsp sugar
salt to taste
1 tablespoon of coriander leaves

Method

1. Wash and cut the aubergines with their stalks left on and slit in half. Place them in a bowl with salted water for half an hour.

2. Mix the rechear masala with half the quantity of finely cut onions and tomato. Mix well and adjust the seasoning by adding a pinch of sugar and salt. Drain the aubergines from the water and wipe them with kitchen paper. Stuff the aubergines with the masala mixture and place them tightly in a bowl.

3. Heat the oil in a pan and fry the remaining onions over a medium heat until soft. Add the tomatoes, green chilli and cook for a minute. Add any remaining rechear masala and two tablespoons of water and vinegar. Simmer gently.

4. Now add the stuffed aubergines to the pan. Cover the pan and cook over very low heat for about 20 minutes or until well done.

5. Lastly, sprinkle with chopped coriander leaves and serve.

Hot and Sour Bitter Gourd - Karela

This recipe is not liked by all, but in Goa it is believed that bitter gourd has several medicinal properties. It is good for the digestive system, diabetes and even the prevention of stomach cancer. Cutting the vegetables into thin slices and applying salt can reduce bitterness.   It should be allowed to stand for an hour or more.

Ingredients

½ lb bitter gourds
1 tsp salt
1 tbsp oil
2 large onion cut into slices
1 large tomato chopped finely
½ tsp of garlic paste (Recipe on page 28)
1 tsp of rechear masala (Recipe on page 30)
1 tbsp of coriander chopped
1 tbsp of vinegar
1 tsp of sugar

Method

1. Scrap the outer knobbly skin of the bitter gourds. Cut the rest lengthwise into half and discard the seeds. Cut them into thin slices and apply salt. Leave them to stand for an hour.   Rinse well and squeeze out the moisture.

2. Heat the oil in a pan and fry the onions till opaque. Add the garlic and tomato. Fry for a minute. Then add the rechear masala and bitter gourds. Stir well to coat the slices of gourd evenly. Add two tablespoon of water and cook gently over a low heat for five minutes.

3. Add the vinegar, sugar, coriander and salt and cook for a further five minutes, stirring occasionally.

This is another easy Chinese recipe. It is delicious and simple to make. Serve with rice and any other Chinese meat or fish dishes.

Ingredients

6 oz walnuts
3 slices canned pineapple
4 spring onions cut into slivers
1 green pepper
1 red pepper
½ medium size onion
4 inch long cucumber piece
1 tomato cut into 8 slices
2 cloves garlic crushed and chopped
3 dessertspoons cooking oil

For the sauce:

4 dtsp white wine vinegar
1½ dtsp sugar
7 dtsp water
2 dtsp tomato ketchup
½ tsp salt
1 tsp cornflour

Method

1. Dice all the vegetables into cubes or long strips.
2. Mix all the sauce ingredients into a bowl.
3. Heat the wok, and then add 2 dessertspoons of cooking oil. When hot add the garlic and stir, then add the green and red pepper and onion, stir until half done. Next add the cucumber, tomato, spring onions and walnuts. Stir again for a minute or two. Mix in the pineapple chunks and the sauce.
4. Stir until the sauce thickens and boils. Mix in 1 dessertspoon of cooking oil and remove from the heat.

Potato and Methi Bhaji

Ingredients

1 lb potatoes boiled, skinned and cut into cubes
2 large onions chopped
1 bunch of fenugreek leaves
1 large tomato cut finely
2 green chillies, de-seeded and cut into small pieces
1 small green pepper cut into small pieces
1 tsp mustard seeds
½ tsp garlic paste
¼ tsp ginger paste
1 ½ tbsp vegetable oil
4 fluid oz of water
salt to taste

Method

1. Discard the stalk of the fenugreek leaves and just select the leaves.
2. Fry the onion until transparent, then add the green chillies and pepper and continue to fry for a minute.
3. Add the mustard seeds and fry until they start crackling, then add tomato and mix well; fry for few seconds. Then put in the garlic and ginger paste and mix well. Simmer for a minute.
4. Add the fenugreek leaves, salt and water to the pan. Cover the pan and cook for 10 minutes.
5. Lastly add the potatoes and simmer on a low heat for five more minutes. Adjust seasoning to taste.

Vegetable Chow Mein – Stir-fried noodles

This recipe can be adapted for prawn or meat Chow Mein, by adding prawns or left-over cooked meat. Similarly different vegetables can achieve a harmonious balance of colour and texture.

Ingredients

1 packet dried Chinese noodles
6 oz bean sprouts, washed and drained
4-6 spring onions, cut into 1½ inch long
½ green or red pepper (or mixture of both) cut into strips
6 button mushrooms sliced
2-3 cloves garlic crushed and chopped
4 dtsp cooking oil
1 tsp corn flour and little water

For the sauce :

1 cup vegetable stock (vegetable cube and warm water}
1 dtsp vegetarian oyster sauce

Method

1. Put the water in a large saucepan and bring it to the boil. Plunge in the noodles and continue to boil until they are tender, but not soggy.

2. Remove and drain them in a colander. Rinse with cold water. Blend the noodles with 1 dessertspoon of cooking oil, mix well and leave aside.

3. Heat the wok until hot, add 1 dessertspoon of cooking oil. When the oil is hot add half the quantity of chopped garlic, swirl around, stir in the pepper and fry for a minute, then add the mushrooms and continue to stir for a further minute. Now add in the bean sprouts and spring onions.

4. Add salt to taste and remove from the heat. Put all the ingredients in the bowl.

5. Clean the wok and re-heat. When hot add 2 dessertspoons of oil, swirl around, add in the remaining garlic, swirl around, add in noodles. Stir and toss until done. Put the noodles in a separate bowl.

6. Once again clean the wok, add the sauce ingredients and bring the sauce to the boil by stirring in continuously. Then add corn flour paste to thicken.

7. Return the noodles, mixed vegetables and cooked meat or prawns to the wok. Stir and toss with the sauce, mix well and serve hot.

Rechear Bendis – Stuffed Ladyfingers

Ingredients

15 ladyfingers
1 tbs rechear masala (Page No.30)
1 small onion cut finely
1 small tomato cut finely
oil for frying
¼ tsp of salt

Method

1. Slit the ladyfingers and apply salt. Set aside.

2. Mix the rechear masala with onion and tomato.

3. Stuff the ladyfingers with the rechear mixture.

4. Heat the frying pan, put a little oil and fry the ladyfingers on a medium heat until soft and limp. Serve as side vegetables.

This is a delicious dish, yet it is simple and quick to make. It holds its shape even when cooked. It can be cooked in different ways.

Ingredients

1 lb of pumpkin (section) peeled and cut into 1 inch / 2 cm cubes
1 pt water
3oz/ 85 gm sugar
1 tbsp soy sauce
½ tsp salt
freshly ground black pepper

Method

1. Place the sugar, water and pumpkin in a saucepan and bring it to the boil.

2. Lower the heat and cover the saucepan with the lid and simmer for about 5 to 6 minutes or until the pumpkin is firm and slightly cooked.

3. Remove the pumpkin with a slotted spoon and leave aside.

4. Boil the vegetable liquid until it is reduced to half the quantity. Add the soy sauce, salt and pepper.

5. Put the pumpkin back in the saucepan and simmer uncovered for about 2 minutes. Allow the pumpkin to cool in the liquid.

6. Reheat before serving.

Roasted Mixed vegetables

Ingredients

2 parsnips, peeled and cut in half lengthways
1 red onion cut into slices
1 large leek cut into 1 inch rounds
1 large red pepper cut in half then cut each half into four pieces lengthways
1 sweet potatoes peeled and cut into 1 inch cubes
1 medium size aubergine cut into 1 inch cubes
3 stems of fresh thyme, chopped
2 tbsp freshly chopped parsley or coriander
4-6 tbsp dripping or olive oil
4 cloves of garlic unpeeled (optional)
Salt and pepper to taste

Method

1. Preheat the oven to Gas Mark 6/200C/400F. Heat the dripping or olive oil in a roasting tray, then add the vegetables and garlic roast for 45 minutes, turning once.

2. Add the thyme and roast for 15 minutes.

3. Remove the vegetables with a slotted spoon and place in the serving dish, season with salt and pepper and serve with sprinkled chopped parsley or coriander.

100

Chick-peas and Spinach Curry

Ingredients

425g /15 oz can of chick-peas drained
1 ½ level tsp garlic and ginger paste
1 large onion, finely chopped
1 green chilli seeded and finely chopped
2 tsp cumin powder
2 tsp ready made curry paste
1 tsp turmeric powder
225g /8oz can of chopped tomatoes
1 green pepper, seeded and chopped
1 ¼ cup vegetable stock
1 tbsp tomato puree
212g/ ½ lb spinach
Salt to taste
3 tbsp chopped coriander

Method

1. Heat the oil in a large saucepan. Add the onion, garlic, ginger and chilli and cook gently until onions are soft and transparent.

2. Stir in the curry paste and cook for a minute. Then add the cumin and turmeric powder and cook gently stirring constantly, so that the flavours are blended together.

3. Add chopped tomatoes and pepper to the pan and stir well. Pour in vegetable stock and stir in tomato puree.

4. Bring it to the boil, lower the heat, cover the pan and simmer 15 minutes.

5. Wash the spinach thoroughly in several change of water. Drain and chop the spinach leaves roughly and add to the pan in small batches.

6. Lastly, add the chick-peas, cover and cook for about 5 – 6 minutes. Stir in fresh coriander, season with salt. Serve with boiled rice, naan, chappatis, raita or chutney.

Cheese and Spring Onion Loaf

Ingredients

250 gm /10 oz self-raising flour
1 teaspoon salt
50 gm/2 oz margarine
4 spring onions finely chopped
4 oz Cheddar cheese, grated
1 small clove of garlic, crushed
1 standard egg beaten
100ml / ¼ pint milk

Method

1. Sieve together the flour and salt. Rub in the margarine. Add the chopped spring onions, cheese and garlic and mix well.   Add the egg and milk and mix to a dough. Knead the dough lightly with your hands, form into the shape of an oblong tube.

2. Well grease a 400gm (1lb) loaf tin. Place the prepared dough in the greased loaf tin. Bake in a moderately hot oven for 1 hour or until golden brown and well risen.

3. Leave in the tin for a few minutes, then turn out on to a wire rack. Serve warm or cold, sliced with butter. Serve with a vegetable soup.

PICKLES, CHUTNEYS AND PRESERVES

Apple Pickle

Apples should be preferably very small and tender cooking apples. When the apples are fully grown then the core and the pips should be discarded.

Ingredients

12 small size green cooking apples
1½ tsp salt
6 cloves of garlic
1 ½ inch ginger
4 tbsp oil
2 fl oz of vinegar
3 tbsp sugar
2 tsp of pickle masala

Method

1. Cut the apples into four pieces and take out the core and the pips.

2. Apply the salt and place them in the bowl under weight for up to three days, making sure that the apples are stirred everyday.

3. On the third day cut the cloves of garlic and ginger in thin slices.

4. Heat the oil in a pan and fry the garlic and ginger very slightly. Remove the pan from the heat.

5. Add the vinegar and bring it to the boil. Then add the sugar and stir until the sugar is dissolved.

6. Lastly, add the apple brine and pickle masala. Bring it to the boil. Simmer on a low heat for 2-3 minutes. Cool the syrup slightly then add the pickled apple pieces. Put the pickle in the clean sterilised jars.

Green Chilly Pickle

Ingredients

12 whole green chillies (possibly large ones, which are less pungent)
6 whole cloves of garlic peeled and cut into halves
1 inch cube fresh ginger peeled and sliced thinly
3 oz malt vinegar
2 tablespoon olive oil
½ teaspoon salt
2 tablespoon sugar
juice and zest of one lime

Method

1. Heat the oil in the saucepan and lower the heat.

2. Put in the garlic and sliced ginger and simmer for a minute. Remove the saucepan from the heat and wait for a few minutes to cool the oil, then add vinegar, salt, sugar, lime juice and zest.

3. Bring it to the boil by stirring the sugar until it is melted. Simmer it on a low heat for five minutes. Add the chillies and simmer for a further one minute. Let it cool before you put it in the sterilised jar. Allow to rest for a couple of weeks before consuming.

Every house in Goa prepares this pickle when the mango season starts. The mangoes should be tender and green and the seed is just forming. Miscut lasts for 6 –9 months. It tastes delicious with pez or canji.

Ingredients

30 tender green mangoes
¾ lb salt
1 tbsp turmeric powder
3 cups sesame seed oil
1 tbsp fenugreek seeds
½ tsp asafoetida (hing)
5 tbsp mustard seeds
5 tbsp chilli powder

Method

1. Wash and wipe the mangoes thoroughly. Cut into four quarters, but do not separate. Remove the seeds carefully and discard them.

2. Sprinkle with the salt and turmeric powder. Mix well. Place in a large container, cover it with a plate and place a 6 kg weight on top. Keep for 2 days, stirring once a day.

3. Heat the oil in a pan until it comes to the boiling point. Put in the fenugreek seeds and remove the pan from the heat. Scoop the fenugreek seeds from the oil and put them in a separate bowl. Allow to cool.

4. Replace the oil pan on the heat. Add the mustard seeds and roast lightly, remove the pan from the heat and put the mustard seeds in the same bowl with fenugreek seeds. Allow to cool.

5. Dry-grind the fenugreek and mustard seeds and add chilli powder, asafoetida and turmeric powder. Mix all these spices in oil.

6. On the third day drain the mangoes and reserve the liquid.

7. Fill each mango with spice mixture and place them in glass jars. Add oil and reserved mango water, making sure that the liquid level is above mangoes. Seal well and allow maturing for about 10-15 days.

Coriander Chutney

Ingredients

3 green chillies
1 tbsp of olive oil
a bunch of fresh coriander washed and chopped
4 spring onions chopped
3 oz /75 g of grated coconut
salt and fresh milled pepper
2 tablespoon vinegar
1 teaspoon sugar

Method

1. Put all the ingredients, except the salt and pepper, into a food processor and switch on to a high speed and blend until the coconut is finely ground into a paste.

2. Sprinkle on the salt and pepper and blend for a minute. Remove the paste and put it in the sterilised bottle.

3. This chutney goes well with cucumber sandwiches. It can remain in the refrigerator for a week.

Sweet Mango Chutney

Ingredients

1 kg semi-ripe mangoes cut into ½ inch cubes
1 lb sugar
1 tbsp finely sliced ginger
1 tbsp finely sliced garlic
1 tsp chilli powder
salt to taste
1½ cup vinegar
1 tbsp mustard seeds
½ lb sultanas

Method

1. In a heavy saucepan boil the mango cubes, vinegar and sugar and cook over a low heat till the sugar melts. Raise the heat to medium and cook till the mangoes are semi-transparent.
2. Add the ginger, garlic, mustard, salt, sultanas and chilli powder to the mango mixture and stir thoroughly. Cook for about 10-15 minutes or until the liquid consistency is thick and the fruit is soft.
3. Cool completely before bottling. Sterilise the jars and bottle the chutney.
4. Do not consume before two weeks. It tastes better when matured.

Mangada – Mango Jam

In Goa mango jam is very popular. During my young days when mangoes were in season my parents would prepare surplus fruit into this mouth-watering jam. We would consume it every morning for breakfast or for a teatime snack. It will preserve for up to one year.

Ingredients

12 cups of mango pulp
6 cups of sugar
2 tbsp of butter (optional)

Method

1. Place in a large and deep saucepan the mango pulp, sugar and butter. Mix thoroughly.
2. Cook over a slow fire, stirring continuously. Bring it to the boil stirring vigorously.
3. The mixture will begin to thicken and when it leaves the sides of the pan the jam is ready. Remove the saucepan from the heat and give one more stir.
4. Cool the mixture and store it in clean and sterilised jars.
5. Alternatively you can prepare the teatime snacks by increasing the sugar contents to 8 cups. Follow the same procedure as above.
6. When ready, pour the mixture on to a greased plate or board and even the edges.
7. When cool, cut them into diamond shapes. Store in an airtight container.

Apple and Tomato Chutney

Ingredients

3 lb tomatoes
3 lb cooking apples, cored
1 lb onions, peeled
1 green pepper
8 oz sultanas
8 oz demerara sugar

½ oz salt
1 inch bruised root ginger
½ oz red chilli powder
2 teaspoons pickling spice
2 pints vinegar

Method

1. Mince together the tomatoes, apples, onions, pepper and sultanas.
2. In a heavy pan place the sugar, salt and spices tied in a muslin cloth, stir in the vinegar and bring it to the boil. Boil gently for about one hour without the lid until the mixture is reduced to a thick consistency.
3. Remove the spice bag, put the mixture through Mouli grater.
4. Place the chutney mixture in the sterilised jars and cover.

Ripe Tomato Chutney

Ingredients

3 lb ripe tomatoes

8 oz onions skinned and chopped finely

12 oz cooking apples

8 oz seedless raisins

1 lb brown sugar

1 oz coarse salt

1½ pints spiced vinegar

Method

1. Dip the tomatoes in the boiling water and skin them.

2. Chop coarsely, removing the stalk ends. Mix the onions and chopped tomatoes.

3. Peel, core and chop the apples. Put the apples, raisins, sugar, salt and vinegar and bring it to the boil.

4. Add the tomatoes and onions and simmer between 45 minutes or one hour. The consistency should be thick.

5. Put the chutney into sterilised and heated jars and cover securely while hot.

Tendli Pickle - Gherkin pickle

Ingredients

100 tendlis

2 cups of oil

10 green chillies minced

4 pods of garlic minced

3 inch piece of ginger minced

1 cup vinegar

1 tablespoon turmeric

2 tablespoons sugar

1 ½ tablespoon chilli powder

1½ tsp salt

Method

1. Cut the tendlis into half then slice them lengthwise.

2. Add the salt and allow to rest for couple of hours.

3. Drain them completely and place in a muslin cloth and let it hang to let the water drain overnight.

4. Put the oil in a saucepan and bring it to the boil, add the green chillies, garlic and ginger. Fry for a minute, then add the vinegar, chilli powder, turmeric, tendlis and sugar.

5. Bring the pickle mixture to the boil over a high heat. Remove from the heat.

6. Sterilise the jars or bottles. Ensure the pickle is covered with oil. If the oil is insufficient then boil a little extra oil and cool it before adding to the bottle.

Lemon Chutney

Ingredients

2 lb lemons
1 lb onions, peeled and chopped
8 oz seedless raisins, washed and dried
2 oz salt
2-2 ½ pints spiced vinegar
½ teaspoon ground ginger
1 ¾ pint white sugar

Method

1. Cut the lemons into half, discard the pips and squeeze juice from the lemons.
2. Chop finely the rind, pith and pulp and mix with the onions and raisins.
3. Pour on lemon juice and salt.
4. Add about 1½ pints of the vinegar or just enough to cover the mixture. Cover and leave overnight.
5. Next·day, turn the mixture into the pan, stir in the ginger, cover and cook gently for about 1 hour till the lemon pieces and onions are quite tender.
6. Add the sugar with the remaining vinegar, and stir vigorously. Boil fast for about 20 minutes till the mixture thickens.
7. Put into hot sterilised j]ars and seal while hot.

Fish Parra - Pickled Salted Fish

This is again a preserve available in every household to be used during the monsoon season, when fresh fish is scarce or unavailable. It is served as an accompaniment to rice and curry dishes. Mackerel is the most common fish used for parra, but dried shark and skate can be used. It takes up to three months to pickle, but it will last for more than 2 years.

Ingredients

1 kg dry salted fish, cut into 3-4" pieces or 25 mackerels cut into halves.

For grinding the parra masala:

60 Kashmiri red chillies
3 inch piece of ginger
2 large pods of garlic
1 tbsp cumin seeds
1 tsp peppercorns
1½ tbsp turmeric powder
1 bottle feni or vodka
2 ½ bottle vinegar
25 cloves of garlic crushed

Method

1. Make the solution of vinegar and water (one part vinegar and three parts water)
2. Wash the fish thoroughly in the vinegar and water solution. Leave aside.
3. Peel and crush the garlic cloves and set aside.
4. Grind the chillies, ginger, garlic, cumin, and peppercorns. (No water should be added)
5. Mix the fish with the ground spices and turmeric powder. The fish should be well coated.
6. Take a clean and sterilised jar and arrange the fish in it, sprinkle the crushed garlic and the remaining ground spices over it.
7. Wash the grinding stone or mixer with vinegar and pour the liquid into the jar.
8. Pour feni or vodka over the parra. Ensure that the fish is completely submerged in spices and vinegar. Cover and store. Allow to pickle for about 4-6 weeks.
9. With a clean and dry spoon remove as much of the parra as you need and shallow fry on both sides for a few minutes.

107

Brinjal Pickle

Ingredients

3 kg brinjals
3 tbsp chilli powder
2 tablespoon turmeric powder
3 tablespoon mustard seeds
1½ tsp salt
2 ¼ cups sugar
5 cups oil
3 tbsp cumin
3 tbsp fenugreek
2 x 4 inch ginger peeled
10 pods of garlic peeled
4¼ cups vinegar
8 curry leaves

Method

1. Remove the stems and cut the brinjals into ½ inch cubes. Put them in a large bowl with salted water. Wash thoroughly and pat dry with kitchen paper, or spread the brinjal cubes on top of a clean cloth.
2. Grind the ginger, garlic, cumin and fenugreek with little vinegar. No water should be used. Mix the spices with chilli and turmeric powder.
3. Heat the oil in a pan, add the mustard seeds and fry until the mustard seeds begin to crackle. Then add the ground spices and fry for 1 or 2 minutes.
4. Add the brinjal cubes, curry leaves, salt and cook on a low heat. Cover the pan and simmer by stirring occasionally until the vegetables are soft.
5. Make the vinegar and sugar solution by dissolving the sugar completely.
6. Add the vinegar solution to the pan and cook until all the moisture evaporates completely. Allow to cool thoroughly.
7. Sterilise the jars and bottle the pickle in airtight jars or bottles, when cool. This pickle will last for more than six months.

Dried Prawn Balchao Preserve

Dried shrimps are plentiful in Goa. Dried shrimp cakes are sold in the market. Local people make preserves in advance to be used during the monsoon season, when fish is scarce or unavailable. This preserve is delicious with fish or Pork Balchao. It can keep for up to six months if stored in airtight jars.

Ingredients

1 kg tiny dried shelled shrimps
2 pods of garlic
6 Kashmiri dried chillies
20 peppercorns
vinegar for grinding
4 curry leaves
½ bottle feni or vodka
½ tsp turmeric
1 tbsp salt
1 cup of oil

Method

1. Wash the shrimps thoroughly and hang in the muslin cloth to drain the water. Put them in the sun to dry.
2. Heat the oil, add a few curry leaves and brown them. Remove and set aside. The oil can be used for any normal cooking.
3. Grind the shrimps, garlic and peppercorns with vinegar. Add the turmeric powder.
4. Pour the shrimp mixture, curry leaves, red chillies, salt, and feni or vodka into a clean and sterilised jar. (the same recipe can be used to make preserve of dry shrimps cakes, only available in Goa).

Coriander and Mint Chutney

This chutney goes well with the cucumber sandwiches or can be eaten with chapattis or naan.

Ingredients

1 bunch of coriander leaves
1 bunch of mint leaves
1 tbsp of tamarind
1 tbsp black gram dal
2 red chillies
½ tsp mustard seeds
¼ tsp of asafoetida powder
1 tsp sugar
2 ½ tbsp vegetable oil
salt to taste

Method

1. Wash thoroughly the coriander and mint leaves. Select the leaves only and discard the stems.

2. Heat a little oil and fry the coriander and mint leaves and keep aside.

3. Heat a tablespoon of oil and fry red chillies and black gram dal.

4. Place the tamarind, chillies and black gram dal in a blender or food processor and blend then add the coriander and mint leaves and grind into a smooth paste. Mix the salt, sugar and asafoetida powder to the chutney mixture.

5. Fry the mustard seeds with the remaining oil until they start to pop then add the chutney mixture and cook on a low heat for about two minutes, stirring constantly.

Pickled Pork Parra – Pickled Salted Pork

Ingredients

2 kg pork (with little fat)
Weak vinegar for washing the meat

Grind the spices in vinegar:

12 Kashmiri dried chillies
1 tsp cumin powder
1 tsp turmeric powder
1 tsp mustard seeds
1 inch piece of ginger
15 cloves of garlic
12 peppercorns
2 tbsp salt

Method

1. Cut the meat into small cubes. Apply the salt and mix well. Set aside, turning twice during the day.

2. Next day wash the meat in weak vinegar (1 part vinegar and 3 parts water)

3. Grind all the spices with vinegar and add to the meat and mix thoroughly.

4. After a few hours mix again.

5. Store in a clean and sterilised jar. The meat should be submerged in vinegar.

6. Use the meat to make 'Chilli fry' as in Recipe for Goan chilly fry.

This pickle can be made instantly during the start of the mango season. It will last for a few days. Raw and tender apples can be substituted for mangoes. It goes well with Pez (canji), or as nibblers.

Ingredients

8 raw mangoes, de-seeded and cut into slivers
2 green chillies cut in half
3 tbsp water
2 tbsp vinegar
1 tsp salt
½ tsp sugar

Method

Take a clean jar and place mangoes and chillies. Add the water, salt, sugar and vinegar to cover the mangoes. Mix well and it is ready to use.

Pork Parra – Spicy Pork Preserve

This recipe again will keep for more than a year in an airtight jar. Be sure to use clean and dry spoon to remove from the jar. The parra can be used as an accompaniment to rice and curry dishes.

Ingredients

4 kg boneless pork with skin and some fat.
6 tablespoon salt
2 tbsp turmeric
1 bottle weak vinegar
(1 part vinegar and 3 parts water)

For grinding the parra masala:

4lb dry Kashmiri red chillies
2 x 3" piece ginger
4 large pods garlic
2 tbsp cumin seeds
2 tsp peppercorns
4 bottles vinegar
1½ bottle feni or vodka
50 cloves of garlic crushed
2 tsp turmeric powder

Method

1. Make slits on the pork (do not cut through).
2. Sprinkle the salt into the slits and all over the pork. It should be well salted.
3. Put the meat in a wicker basket and place some weight on it. Place the wicker basket on top of any earthenware to collect the water from the meat. Allow to rest for a day. The water drained from the pork should be discarded.
4. Next day sprinkle the turmeric powder over the pork and spread it on a clean tray to dry in the sun for 4 - 5 days. It should be completely dry.
5. Cut each slit to make slabs of meat. Then cut again to whatever size the jar will hold.
6. Grind the parra masala and add 2 tablespoons of turmeric powder. Mix well. Wash the grinding stone or mixer with vinegar and reserve the masala liquid.
7. Take a wide-mouthed glass or earthen jar, place the pork pieces in it then sprinkle the crushed garlic, ground spices and masala-reserved liquid over them.
8. Now fill the jar with fini or vodka. Ensure that the pork is completely submerged in spices and vinegar. Cover the mouth of the jar tightly and store. Allow to rest for 4-6 weeks. The meat will be pickled and ready to use.
9. To serve, remove the meat from the jar with clean and dry spoon. Cut into small pieces and fry in oil until tender. Alternatively, you can boil it with a little water and roughly sliced onions until all the water is absorbed and the meat is slightly fried with its own fat.

110

Fish Mole

Various types of fish can be used for this recipe, such as prawns, mussels, mackerels and kingfish. It is usually prepared when fish is cheap and plentiful and used when fish is scarce during the monsoon season. It keeps well over six months. Serve with rice and curry.

Ingredients

3 kg prawns shelled or mussels
20 cloves of garlic peeled and cut into thin slices
2 tsp turmeric powder
8 fl oz / 1 cup feni or vodka
2 tsp cumin powder
8 fl oz /1 cup vinegar
2 pints / 4 cups oil
salt to taste

Spices for grinding in vinegar:

20 cloves garlic
25 dried red chillies
1 inch piece ginger

Method

1. Wash the prawns and apply salt. Set aside.
2. Fry the prawns well and put to dry in the sun for half a day.
3. Heat the oil, add the garlic slices and cook briefly.
4. Add the ground and powdered spices and vinegar.
5. Bring it to the boil. Then add the feni and set aside to cool.
6. Add the prawns and mix well.
7. Store in airtight and sterilised bottles.

The same recipe is used for mussels, but the method for mackerel is that the fish should be cut into half or three pieces if the mackerel is very large. King fish should be cut into slices.

Chepnim Toram - Raw Mangoes in Brine

This goes well with canji or rice and curry. It can be kept for well over six months or a year.

Ingredients

30 tender small green mangoes (with soft seeds)
2 cups of coarse sea salt
6 dried red Kashmiri chillies
½ tsp asafoetida powder (hing)

Method

1. Wash the mangoes and wipe them dry. Leave them whole.
2. Place them in a large earthenware/porcelain basin. Sprinkle some salt at the bottom.
3. Arrange the mangoes, chillies and asafoetida. After every layer sprinkle some salt. Place a small plate on top of the mangoes and keep some weight on it so that the mangoes are pressed down. Cover the basin with a muslin cloth. Allow to marinate in salt for three days.
4. Everyday the mangoes should be turned over and sprinkled with a little more salt. Replace the weight and cover.
5. Repeat the process for three days and you will observe that a lot of liquid is accumulated.
6. Transfer the mangoes with the brine into a glass jar, ensuring that they are completely submerged in the brine. Allow to mature for at least 2 weeks.
7. Always ensure that the mangoes are removed from the jar with a dry slotted spoon, so that the remaining mangoes are covered in the brine.

Aramit's Sweet Lime Pickle

This is my favourite pickle recipe given to me by my aunt Aramit. She prepares it with great care and enthusiasm. The longer it matures the better it tastes. It can last for up to a year or more.

Ingredients

12 limes cut into one inch cubes
juice of 3 limes
3 x 1 inch piece of ginger
1 tsp turmeric powder
6 cloves of garlic cut into quarters
1½ tsp black powder
½ cup of grated jaggery
1 tbsp salt
4 tbsp groundnut oil
1 tsp mustard seeds
1 tsp fenugreek
½ tsp asafoetida powder

Method

1. Place the lemon cubes, garlic and ginger in earthenware and sprinkle on the salt. Mix in the lemon juice and stir well. Cover it with the lid. Place some weight on the lid and keep for up to three days, ensuring that the limes cubes mixture is turned daily.

2. On the third day heat the oil in a pan and add the mustard seeds and fry until they crackle, then add the fenugreek, asafoetida powder, the brine of lime mixture and bring it to the boil.

3. Add the grated jaggery, turmeric powder and pepper. Stir gently in reduced flame until the jaggery dissolves completely and looks like syrup. Add the lime cubes. Remove from the fire and allow cooling. Store it in a dry sterilised bottle. Allow to mature for at least 2- 3 weeks.

Aubergine Chutney

This recipe was given to me by an old friend, Michael Fernandes of Oxford, who is an expert in preparing Goan chutneys and pickles. It is prepared with great care and enthusiasm and delicious to taste.

Ingredients

1.5kg/3lb3oz aubergines cut into cubes
28gm/1oz turmeric powder
9 cloves of garlic peeled
2 inches root ginger peeled
28gm/1 oz fenugreek seeds
28gm/1oz mustard seeds
1pt/16fl oz malt vinegar
1pt/16fl oz extra virgin olive oil
230gm/8 oz caster sugar
230gm/8 oz sultanas
57gm/ 2oz dried red chillies, discard seeds
1 ½ tsp salt
1 tsp dried tamarind

Method

1. Place the aubergine cubes in a large bowl and apply salt and leave it rest for about 30 minutes.

2. Grind the ginger, garlic, chillies and tamarind with vinegar into smooth paste, then add the powdered spices (turmeric, fenugreek and mustard).

3. Heat the oil in a heavy pan, add the ground masala and fry for a minute, then add the vinegar and sugar and cook on a low heat until the sugar is dissolved completely.

4. Squeeze the liquid from the aubergine cubes and pat dry with kitchen paper.

5. Now add the aubergines and cook for 10-15 minutes, stirring occasionally.

6. Lastly, add the chopped curry leaves and cook for a couple of minutes.

7. Allow the mixture to cool thoroughly. Then bottle the chutney in the sterilised and airtight jars ensuring that the oil is slightly above the chutney mixture.

SALADS

Goan Cabbage Salad

This recipe is widely used in Goan restaurants and households. It is simple and quick to make and ready to use within an hour. It tastes sharper when left for few days in the bottle. It can be kept for a week and used with any bean dishes or as side salad.

Ingredients

1 lb finely shredded cabbage
3 small carrots, trimmed, peeled and
cut into long julienne strips (4 cm long)
2-3 long hot green chillies de-seeded and
cut into 4 cm long thin strips
6 fl oz of Goa vinegar or white wine vinegar
2 tbsp of water
1 tbsp salt
1 tsp sugar

Method

1. Put the shredded cabbage, carrots and green chillies into a large clean, wide-mouthed jar.

2. Place the vinegar, salt, water and sugar in the bowl and mix thoroughly until the salt and sugar are dissolved.

3. Pour the mixture into the jar and mix again with a clean spoon.

4. Cover and leave for an hour.

Pineapple and Avocado Salad

Ingredients

1 ripe pineapple
2 ripe avocado
2 large oranges
3 oz / 75 g rocket leaves
1 medium size red onion, cut into thin rings

For the dressing:

5 tbsp / 75 ml olive oil
2 tbsp / 30 ml lemon juice
Salt and black pepper

Method

1. Cut off the top-notch of the pineapple and strip off the skin by cutting thin strips from the top to the bottom of the fruit, making sure that the eyes are cut off.

2. Cut the pineapple in half lengthwise then cut each pineapple half into ten slices.

3. Halve the avocados and remove the stones. Carefully peel off the skin, then cut each avocado half lengthwise into six slices.

4. Peel the oranges and cut out the segments, cutting either side of the dividing membranes.

5. Combine the dressing ingredients in a small bowl and mix well.

6. Assemble the salad on a large oval serving platter. Alternate slices of pineapple, avocado and oranges. Add a handful of rocket leaves and onion rings. Spoon over the dressing and serve immediately.

Indian Carrot Salad

Ingredients

1 lb carrots peeled and grated
salt to taste
2 tbsp vegetable oil
1½ tsp whole black mustard seeds
½ tsp clear honey, mixed with 1 tbsp of warm water

Method

1. In a large bowl, toss the grated carrots and salt.

2. Heat the oil in a small frying pan and when hot put in the mustard seeds.

3. When the mustard seeds begin to pop, add the honey mixture and mix thoroughly. Pour the contents of the frying pan over the carrots. Mix well and serve.

Cabbage with Carrots and Spring Onions

Ingredients

1 lb green cabbage cut into long strips
1 carrot
2 spring onions
2 fl oz vegetable oil
1 tsp salt
1 tbsp sherry wine
½ inch long ginger cut into very fine strips
½ tsp mustard seeds

Method

1. Discard the coarse outer leaves and the hard core of the cabbage, then cut it into long strips.

2. Peel the carrot and cut into julienne strips.

3. Cut the spring onions into long strips.

4. Heat the oil in the wok over a medium flame. When hot put in the ginger. Stir and fry for about 30 seconds, then add the mustard seeds and fry until they begin to crackle. Put in the vegetables and salt.

5. Stir and fry for 3 minutes. Add the wine and cook for further 3-4 minutes or until the cabbage is tender enough to eat, but still retains some of its crispness.

Fresh Apple and Peach Salad

This is a wonderful salad to make when fresh fruits are in season. It should be made just before you sit down to have your meal. It can be served as an appetiser or side salad dish.

Ingredients

1 lb fresh peaches peeled and sliced
2 eating apples cored, peeled and sliced
2 tsp sugar
½ tsp salt
freshly ground pepper to taste
1½ tsp ground roasted cumin seeds
juice of one lemon
½ tsp cayenne pepper
1 tbsp water

Method

1. Combine the peaches and apples in a salad bowl. Place in a small bowl the lemon juice, water, salt, sugar, cumin seeds and cayenne pepper. Mix thoroughly until the sugar is dissolved. Pour the dressing over the salad and serve immediately at room temperature.

Gajjar and Moli Salad - Carrot and White Radish Salad

Ingredients

2 large carrots
1 large white radish
½ tsp salt
1 tbsp sesame oil
1 tbsp rice vinegar
¼ tsp light soy sauce
¼ tsp sugar
pinch of cayenne powder

Method

1. Wash the carrots and radish thoroughly.

2. Peel the carrots and cut into thin diagonal slices. Cut each slice into julienne strips.

3. Peel the radish and cut it into julienne strips about the same size as the carrot strips.

4. Put the carrots and radish in a bowl. Add the salt and mix well. Let it rest for an hour.

5. Drain thoroughly, pressing out as much as liquid as possible.

6. Put the vegetables in a serving bowl. Add the sesame oil, vinegar, soy sauce, sugar and cayenne powder. Mix well.

Yoghurt with Roasted Aubergine

Ingredients

3 spring onions
1 large sized aubergine about 1lb in weight
1 clove garlic peeled and mashed to a pulp
3 tbsp finely chopped fresh mint
2 tbsp olive oil
2 tbsp natural yoghurt
1 tbsp salad cream
freshly ground black pepper
iced water

Method

1. Cut the spring onions into very fine rounds using only the tender soft sections. Put them in a bowl and pour iced water over it and refrigerate for an hour.

2. Prick the aubergine in several places with a fork. Roast it under the grill on a low heat, do not allow it to burn. As it gets charred on one side, turn the aubergine slightly, using a pair of tongs. Roast the entire aubergine. When it is done, it will appear very limp.

3. Peel the aubergine under cold running water and leave it to drain in a colander for a few minutes. Then finely chop the flesh.

4. Put the yoghurt and salad cream in a bowl and beat lightly with a fork or a whisk until smooth and creamy.

5. Add the aubergine, garlic, mint, salt, olive oil and black pepper.

6. Drain the spring onions and pat dry with kitchen paper. Add them to the yoghurt and mix. Serve at room temperature or chilled.

Ripe Tomatoes and Mango Salad

Ingredients

½ lb ripe large tomatoes
1 tsp coarsely grated fresh ginger
half ripe mango peeled and cut into thin slices
3 spring onions cut into julienne strips
1 tsp lemon juice
½ red onion sliced into rings
1 tbsp vegetable oil
sugar to taste
freshly ground black pepper and salt
1 tbsp chopped coriander

Method

1. Cut the tomatoes into thick rounds and arrange them in a single layer on a platter.

2. Sprinkle the ginger, mango slices, red onion rings and spring onions evenly over the tomatoes.

3. Blend the oil, lemon juice, salt and pepper in a small bowl and shake vigorously. Add the sugar and mix thoroughly again. Pour the dressing over the salad just before serving. Garnish with the chopped coriander.

Mixed Bean Salad

Ingredients

3 oz black-eyed beans
3 oz kidney beans soaked in water for couple of hours
4 oz French beans
3 spring onions cut into fine rounds including green leaves
4 tbsp olive oil
1½ pt water
½ tsp salt
3 tbsp lemon juice
freshly ground black pepper
2 tbsp finely chopped fresh parsley

Method

1. Put the black-eyed and kidney beans in a heavy pan with water. Bring to the boil.

2. Cover the pan and simmer on a low heat for two minutes.

3. Turn off the heat and let the pan remain covered for an hour.

4. Uncover and bring it to the boil again.

5. Cover, and simmer gently for 40 minutes or until the beans are tender, but still retain their shape. Alternatively, you can buy a tin of processed mixed beans.

6. Remove the ends from the French beans and cook in the boiling water for about 4-5 minutes. Drain and set aside to cool, and then cut the French beans into quarters.

7. Mix the French beans and pulses in a large salad bowl and add the spring onions.

8. Prepare the salad dressing in a small bowl with the olive oil, lemon juice, salt and pepper. Shake vigorously. Pour the dressing over the beans while they are still hot. Adjust seasoning.

Couscous Salad with Almonds and Preserved Lemon

Ingredients

9 oz couscous
3 tbsp raisins
16 fl oz of boiling water
3 tbsp olive oil
3 shallots finely chopped
1 clove of garlic
1 tbsp sherry vinegar
2 tbsp capers
2 oz toasted flaked almonds
3 preserved lemon quarters
Handful of parsley and mint finely chopped

Method

1. Place the couscous and raisins into a bowl and pour the boiling water over them, adding two tablespoons of the olive oil.

2. Stir and leave aside for five minutes until the couscous has absorbed all the liquid.

3. Meanwhile, sauté the shallots and garlic in the remaining oil.

4. Fluff up the grains with a fork.

5. Finely chop the preserved lemons.

6. Add to the couscous along with the shallot mixture, preserved lemons, sherry vinegar, capers and almonds.

7. Season with salt and stir in the chopped herbs.

8. Serve at room temperature.

Raita with Cucumber

This is a popular Indian salad and served with dal and spicy curries. The Raita is refreshing and deliciously cool after a hot spicy meal.

Ingredients

½ cucumber chopped finely
1 onion chopped finely
2 tbsp of fresh coriander chopped
12 fl oz of natural yogurt
1 green chilli de-seeded and cut finely
salt and freshly ground pepper
pinch of paprika
1 tbsp mayonnaise
a sprig of fresh mint

Method

1. In a large salad bowl, place the chopped cucumber, onion, chilli and coriander. Mix well.

2. In a separate bowl beat the yoghurt lightly then add the yoghurt mixture to the salad bowl. Mix thoroughly and adjust seasoning by adding salt and pepper. Mix again and sprinkle with the paprika. Garnish with mint leaves. Serve as an accompaniment to rice and curry dishes.

Roast Tomato, Rocket and Feta Salad

This can be served as a first course or as a side salad with grilled fish or roast chicken.

Ingredients

2 tbsp extra virgin olive oil
1 lb plum tomatoes, halved lengthways
3 cloves garlic, not peeled (optional)
1 big sprig of fresh thyme
salt and freshly ground black pepper
a pinch of sugar
1 tbsp white wine vinegar
handfuls of fresh rocket
110g/4oz feta cheese, diced or crumbled
a few fresh basil leaves, roughly torn

Method

1. Preheat the oven to Gas Mark 7/ 220C/ 425F.

2. Grease a roasting tin generously with extra virgin oil.

3. Arrange the plum tomato halves in it, cut sides up, and tuck the garlic and thyme among them

4. Drizzle over a tablespoon of olive oil, then season with salt, freshly ground black pepper and a pinch of sugar.

5. Roast for about 40-45 minutes, until very tender and patched here and there with brown specks.

6. Remove from the oven, cool and reserve until needed.

7. Make a quick dressing by whisking the remaining oil with vinegar, salt and freshly ground black pepper.

8. Taste and adjust the balance of flavours, adding a little more oil if it is on the sharp side. Reserve.

9. Just before serving, toss the rocket leaves in enough dressing to coat and then top with the feta cheese and roasted tomatoes (and cloves of garlic, if you wish).

10. Drizzle over some of the juice from the roasting tin and sprinkle with fresh basil leaves.

DESSERTS

Bibinca

Ingredients

3 cups sugar
½ cup water
10 cardamoms (crushed)
10 eggs (yolks only)
2 cups coconut milk (thick)
1 cup plain flour
½ cup melted ghee

Method

1. Make thin syrup of the sugar, water and cardamoms. Cool and strain.
2. Beat the egg yolks and add the coconut milk, flour and the cooled syrup. Keep standing for an hour before baking.
3. Heat the ovenproof dish and when hot put in a tablespoon of ghee and place in the oven on high heat. The ghee should be bubbling hot.
4. Pour in a little batter to form a layer. Cook till brown.
5. Pour another tablespoon of ghee over this layer and place it under the grill on medium heat. When it is hot, add another layer of batter. Cook until it is brown.
6. Continue the process until all the batter has been used.

Note: If you prefer layers to be of different colours, food colouring can be used by dividing the batter into two or three different colours.

Potato Bibinca

Ingredients

½ kg potatoes
350 ml / ½ cup water
6 eggs
180g / 1½ cups sugar
4 tablespoon plain flour
2 tbsp semolina
1 pt / 2 cups of coconut milk
6 level tablespoon butter
8 cardamoms (crushed into powder)

Method

1. Boil the potatoes, mash and set aside.
2. Make syrup of the sugar, then cool and set aside.
3. Mix the flour and semolina with a little coconut milk and blend in the yolks of the eggs, one at a time, beating lightly after each addition.
1. Add the boiled mashed potatoes and the rest of the coconut milk.
2. Then add the whites of the eggs (well beaten).
3. Heat the ghee in a pan, pour in the batter and bake. If preferred, bake in layers, as given in recipe 'Bebinca' on page 194.

This is my mother-in-law's recipe. These fritters taste delicious when hot and should be served immediately after cooking. My grandson Ben loves them.

Ingredients

3 fully ripe bananas
5 oz white plain flour
4 fl oz milk
1 tbsp sugar
a pinch of cinnamon powder
salt to taste
6 tps of ghee or unsalted butter for shallow frying

Method

1. Make a batter with the flour and milk then add the salt and sugar.

2. Peel the bananas and mash them well into soft consistency.

3. Mix the banana mash into the batter and add ½ teaspoon of bicarbonate of soda. Leave aside for an hour to rise.

4. Heat the frying pan, then put 2 tablespoons of ghee and make sure that the oil is very hot. Place two tablespoons of batter and fry until they turn into] golden brown. They should be served immediately.

Doce De Grao – Gram Sweet with coconut

This is a well loved Festive sweet, prepared especially during Christmas season. Every household in Goa will prepare this sweet. It can keep for weeks if stored in an air-tight jar.

Ingredients

½ kg Bengal gram (channa dal) washed and soaked over night
½ kg sugar
1½ pt / 3 cups of water
½ coconut, grated and finely ground
1 tablespoon ghee (clarified butter)
a pinch of salt
6 cardamoms (powdered)

Method

1. Cook the dal with 3 cups of water in a pan. It should be tender and almost dry. Grind finely in the mixer.

2. Make a fairly thick syrup with the sugar and one cup of water. Cool till lukewarm.

3. Stir in the ground dal and coconut and cook over a medium heat, stirring constantly.

4. As the mixture begins to thicken, add the ghee, a spoonful at a time.

5. Keep on stirring and do not allow to stick.

6. When the mixture begins to leave the sides of the pan, add the salt and powdered cardamoms depending on the taste of the individual. The mixture can be cooked to a soft stage, but does not last too long. The mixture cooked to a very hard stage will keep for weeks.

7. Stir well and place the mixture onto a flat dish coated lightly with margarine or ghee. Mark with a sharp knife in a criss-cross design. Allow to cool. Cut into individual pieces and store in an airtight tin.

Goan Tropical Fruit Salad

This popular fruit salad makes an excellent light dessert. It is refreshing and delicious to eat, after a rich spicy meal.

Ingredients

½ pineapple, peeled, cored and diced
1 large mango, peeled, stoned and cubed
juice of 2 large oranges
juice of 1 lime
2 satsumas or mandarins, peeled and segmented
1 chickoo or kiwi fruit, peeled and cut into round slices
2 passion fruits
2 ripe bananas, peeled and cut into rounds
2 oz red and green seedless grapes
½ pomegranate (optional)
½ small galia melon
1 tsp sugar
½ tsp freshly grated nutmeg
1 small wine glass of sherry
6 fl oz of tropical fruit juice

Method

1. Place the pineapple, mango, chickoo, or kiwi, bananas and grapes in a large fruit salad bowl.

2. In a separate bowl put the orange, lemon and the tropical fruit juice, then add the sugar, wine and nutmeg powder. Stir vigorously until the sugar is dissolved. Add the mixture to the fruit salad bowl.

3. Halve the melon lengthwise and scoop out all the seeds. Then cut into wedges and remove the skin. Now cut the wedges into dainty bite-size pieces and add to the salad bowl.

4. Cut the passion fruit into half, then scoop out all the contents of the fruit and add to the fruit bowl. Discard the outer shell. Decorate the fruit salad with a sprig of mint.

Bramley Apple Cake

Ingredients

8 oz castor sugar
2 large eggs
4 oz butter
7 oz /175g plain flour
4 fl oz milk or single cream
3 tsp baking powder
3-4 Bramley cooking apples
1 oz brown sugar to sprinkle over the apples

Method

1. Grease and flour an 8 x 12 inches roasting tin.

2. Whisk the eggs and sugar until the mixture is thick and creamy. Make sure that the whisk leaves a trail when it is lifted out.

3. Put the butter and milk into a pan. Bring it to the boil and stir.

4. While the milk is still boiling, pour into the eggs and sugar.

5. Sieve in the flour and baking powder and fold carefully into the batter, so that there are no lumps of flour.

6. Pour the mixture into the prepared roasting tin.

7. Peel, core and slice the apples and arrange them over the batter.

8. Sprinkle with one ounce of castor sugar.

9. Bake in a moderately hot oven at Gas Mark 6 /200C/ 400 F for 25-30 minutes until well-risen and golden brown.

10. Cool in the tin then cut into slices.

Apple and Raspberry Cheesecake

Ingredients

4 oz /125g digestive biscuits
1½ oz/40g butter melted
3 large Bramley cooking apples, peeled, cored and sliced.
3 oz/90g fresh raspberries
4 tbsp /60g granulated sugar
½ tsp cinnamon powder
7oz/ 170g fromage frais
1 tbsp caster sugar
2 eggs

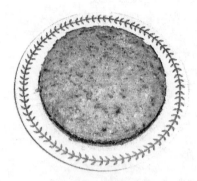

Method

1. Crush the digestive biscuits into smooth crumbs and reserve a tablespoon of biscuits crumbs for later use.

2. Mix the rest of the biscuits crumbs with the melted butter. Press into the base of a 6 inch/15cm loose-bottomed flan case and chill it for 30 minutes.

3. Place the sliced apples in the saucepan with the cinnamon powder and two tablespoons of sugar and bring it to the boil. Simmer on a low fire, stirring occasionally until the apples are well cooked and resemble like apple sauce.

4. In a separate saucepan cook the raspberries with two tablespoon sugar until all the liquid evaporates and the sauce is thick and smooth.

5. Pre-heat the oven to Gas Mark 5 190C/375F.

6. Spread two-thirds of the apple sauce in the prepared tin; then two-thirds of the raspberry sauce over it.

7. Mix the remaining apple and raspberry puree with the fromage frais, sugar and eggs. Pour the mixture over the raspberry sauce.

8. Bake the cheesecake for an hour. Cool for 5 minutes before removing from the tin and sprinkle with the reserve crumbs. Serve hot or cold.

Carrot Cake Indian Style

Ingredients

1½ tsp vegetable oil
128g /4½ oz plain white flour including flour for dusting
1 tsp bicarbonate of soda
¼ tsp salt
2 large eggs
¼ tsp ground cardamom powder
227g / 8 oz granulated sugar
57g / 2 oz unsalted butter
340g / 12 oz grated carrots
2 tbsp chopped pistachios
2 tbsp blanched almonds
2 tbsp raisins

Method

1. Brush a non-stick 9 inches cake tin with the vegetable oil, then dust it lightly with flour.

2. Sift the flour with the bicarbonate of soda and salt.

3. Beat the eggs well in a large bowl. Add the cardamom powder, sugar and butter. Keep beating until all the ingredients are thoroughly mixed.

4. Add the sifted flour mixture to the ingredients in the bowl and fold it in gently with a spatula.

5. Add the carrots, pistachios, almonds, and raisins. Fold them in gently.

6. Preheat the oven to a temperature at Gas Mark 4/180C /350F.

7. Place the cake batter into the oiled and floured cake tin and bake in the preheated oven for 35 to 40 minutes or until a skewer inserted inside comes out clean and the top is golden red in colour.

This is my eldest son's favourite recipe. It is simple and quick to make. He often serves us this dessert after his delicious Indian meal and we all enjoy it very much.

Ingredients

6 ripe bananas
¼ pint or 150 ml dark rum
double cream for serving (optional)

The syrup:

Juice of 2 oranges
Grated rind of ½ orange
2 oz (50g) castor sugar
2 oz (50g) butter

Method

1. First make the syrup: Put the orange juice, rind, sugar and butter into a 9 in (23cm) omelette pan. Heat, stirring constantly, over a moderate heat until boiling.

2. Simmer for 5 minutes. Remove and set aside.

3. Peel the bananas and carefully place them in the syrup. Simmer for 2 minutes. Turn and cook on the second side for 2 minutes.   Set the pan aside on a heat proofed mat.

4. Take a small saucepan and pour the rum into it. Warm briefly over a low heat.

5. At the table: set the pan of syrup over a lighted spirit lamp. Set alight the rum and pour over the bananas.

6. Serve as soon as the flames die down, with the syrup spooned over.

7. Pass the cream separately, if using it.

Bulinas - Semolina Biscuits

Ingredients

450g / ½ kg semolina
6 egg yolks
2 coconuts grated or 2 cups of desiccated coconut
450g / ½ kg sugar (according to your taste)
½ cup water
1 tsp vanilla essence

Method

1. Grind the grated coconuts finely.

2. Mix the sugar and water and cook until smooth syrup is formed.

3. Add the ground coconut and stir well.

4. Cook for 3-4 minutes then set aside to cool.

5. Add the egg yolks and mix thoroughly.

6. Add the semolina and essence and mix well. Form the mixture into small balls.

7. Place the bulinas in the prepared greased tins and bake in the pre-heated oven at Gas Mark 4/ 180C/ 350F for 30-40 minutes or until they are golden brown.

8. Remove from the tins and cool. Store in airtight jars.

Neureos

Ingredients

1 lb plain flour
2 tbsp ghee
water for kneading
oil for deep frying
salt to taste

Ingredients for the filling:

1 coconut finely grated (or equal portions of coconut and semolina)
4 oz cashew nuts finely chopped
¼ tsp cardamoms powder
½ lb sugar
2 tbsp ghee
4 oz raisins, finely chopped
2 oz of cherries
1 oz of sesame seeds
4 fl oz / ½ cup water

Method

1. Heat the sugar and water to make syrup. Add the coconut, nuts and ghee.
2. Keep stirring vigorously. When the mixture dries, add the raisins, cherries, sesame seeds and cardamom powder. Remove from the heat and allow to cool.
3. Mix the flour, salt, water and ghee, then knead into soft dough. Cover and set aside for half an hour.
4. Divide the dough into small balls and roll out each ball into a thin layer of pastry.
5. Cut out circles of 4 inch in diameter. Place a spoonful of filling in the middle of the circle. Wet the edge of each circle with water, roll one half over to make a semi-circle and press edges firmly to seal. Trim the edges with a pastry-cutter and press them with a fork or knife to make designs.
6. Deep fry until light brown in colour. Cool and store in an airtight container.

Kol – Kol

Ingredients

½ kg white plain flour
1 cup coconut milk (thick)
2 eggs (beaten)
1 tbsp butter for kneading
8 cardamoms peeled and powdered
1 tbsp caster sugar
¼ tsp salt
oil for deep frying

Method

1. Knead the flour and the coconut milk, add the eggs, sugar, cardamom powder, salt and enough butter to make a pliable dough.
2. Cover the dough and leave it to stand for 15 minutes.
3. Take a small quantity of the dough and roll it into a ball. Shape the ball over the fork, then roll one end to form a cylinder. Continue the process until all the dough is used up.
4. Put the oil in a heavy pan and bring it to the boiling point.
5. Turn the heat to a medium temperature then deep fry them till light brown, turning them over once.
6. These Kol-Kol can be served as it is or dip them in the sugar syrup when cooled.

Dodol

Ingredients

1 ½ large coconut grated
4 oz/125 gm rice flour
8 oz /230 gm jaggery
2 oz /57 gm almonds or cashew nuts blanched and chopped
salt to taste

Method

1. Grind the coconut and extract one cup of thick coconut juice and set aside.

2. Add more water and extract the thin juice. Mix the flour with the thin juice. Place the mixture in the saucepan, add the salt and bring it to the boil. Add half the quantity of jaggery and continue boiling, stirring all the time. As the mixture thickens, add the remaining jaggery and keep stirring.

3. Add the thick coconut juice and continue to boil stirring vigorously. Add the nuts. When the mixture begins to leave the sides of the saucepan and oil begins to ooze out, the dodol is ready.

4. Pour the dodol into a flat serving dish and spread it evenly. Cut into diamond or square shapes when cool.

Ale Bele - Coconut crepes

Ingredients

For crepes:

125 gm (1½ cup) plain white flour
pinch of baking powder
¼ tsp salt
1 egg
1 tbsp granulated sugar
120 ml / ½ cup milk
120 ml / ½ cup water

For the filling:

3 tbsp sugar or jaggery dissolved in 1 tbsp water over a low heat
160g /2 cups grated fresh coconut
margarine for frying

Method

1. Mix all the dry ingredients together in a bowl.

2. Beat the egg with the sugar till frothy. Mix in the milk and water.

3. Pour the liquid gradually into the flour mixture and stir vigorously. Beat well for a minute or two. There should not be any lumps.

4. Allow to rest for 20 minutes.

5. Grease a 6 inch frying pan lightly with margarine and heat then pour two tablespoon of batter into it. Tilt the frying pan to coat the base evenly. Cover and cook for a minute.

6. Remove the pancake from the frying pan and place it on a plate. Repeat the process till all the batter is used up.

7. For the filling: In a separate pan add the sugar/ jaggery syrup and coconut, cook for a few seconds. Allow to cool.

8. Place a little filling on each pancake and roll lightly.

9. Serve with any left-over filling mixture.

Ras Malai

Ingredients

2 litres milk
150g /1¼ cup sugar
960ml / 4 cups water
juice of one lemon
4 almonds blanched, skinned and cut into small pieces
½ tsp rose water or essence

Method

1. Boil one litre of milk till it reduces to one-third of its quantity. Add ¼ cup of sugar, the almonds pieces and rose water and keep aside.
2. Boil the other litre of milk and add lemon juice to it. When the milk curdles, remove from the heat and strain through a muslin cloth.
3. Tie the muslin cloth and hang it for 15 minutes to drain the excess liquid completely.
4. Knead the mixture well until it turns into a smooth paste. The smoother the paste, the better the sweet will taste.
5. Form into small balls and flatten them. Keep aside.
6. Heat 4 cups of water with one cup of sugar. Allow the sugar to dissolve and keep boiling.
7. Now gently drop the flattened balls into it. Cover and cook for 30 minutes.
8. Turn them over and cook for 10 more minutes on a low heat.
9. Remove the pan from the heat with the syrup and leave them to rest for 20 minutes.
10. Gently remove the balls from the syrup and put them in the cream milk.

Sanna - Goan Steamed Rice Bread

This is a delicious bread prepared in Goa on special occasions. It is served traditionally with sorpatel, but can be eaten with any other gravy dishes. In Goa toddy (fresh sap of the coconut palm) is used as a raising agent, which brings out an exotic taste. If toddy is unavailable it can be substituted with active dry yeast.

Ingredients

1½ cup /300 gm raw parboiled rice
50 gm grated coconut
¾ tsp active dry yeast
or 1½ cup / 360 ml toddy
2 tbsp / 30 gm sugar
salt to taste

Method

1. Wash and soak the rice overnight or for at least 8 hours. Drain and grind with coconut and a little water.
2. If using yeast, mix in a bowl 1 teaspoon sugar and half a cup of warm water. Sprinkle the yeast over it and mix well. Leave it to stand in a warm place for few minutes to froth. In a separate bowl mix together the ground rice-coconut paste, sugar, salt and toddy or yeast mixture to make a thick batter. If using yeast, enough water will have to be added to make thick batter. Cover the bowl and leave the batter to rise in a warm place for at least 4 hours or till the batter doubles in volume.
3. Grease the small steaming moulds. Pour a little batter in each mould, leaving enough room for it to rise. Place the moulds in a steamer and steam for 10-15 minutes till fluffy but cooked through.

Coilorio – Goan rice bread

This is Goan rice bread or can be eaten as teatime snack. It is delicious and wholesome. It can be made a few days in advance. Re-heat and serve.

Ingredients

½ kg Goa rice or raw rice
1 grated coconut
2 cups / 1 pint of water to extract juice
250 gm grated jaggery
1 egg
ghee or margarine to fry
pinch of cardamom powder
salt to taste

Method

1. Wash and soak the rice overnight. Grind the coconut with water and extract the juice.
2. Grind the rice with half of the coconut juice. Mix the jaggery and salt and set aside.
3. In a separate bowl beat the egg until the mixture is frothy, then add the remaining coconut juice, rice mixture and cardamom powder and beat it thoroughly to make a thick batter.
4. Heat some ghee or margarine in a deep frying-pan and put two tablespoons of batter in it. Fry for a minute or two then turn over on the other side until it is brown on both sides. Remove the coilorio and drain on the kitchen paper.

Chapatti – Unleavened Indian bread

This recipe is widely used in most of the Indian households. Chapattis are made out of finely ground wheat meal flour known as ata or chapatti flour. It is available in all Indian grocery stores. There are several other Indian breads that can be prepared from this flour; i.e parathas, roti, naan and pooris. Alternatively, you can use half the quantity of wheat meal and plain flour.

Ingredients

8 oz / 230g chapatti flour
½ tsp salt
4 tbsp margarine or ghee (melted)
2 tbsp vegetable oil
6 fl oz of water
additional flour for dusting

Method

1. Put the flour and salt in a large bowl. Pour the oil over the flour and rub it in with your fingertips.
2. Add the water and gather the dough together in a ball. You should end up with soft dough. Knead the dough for about 8 – 10 minutes and make it into a large ball.
3. Put the dough back in the bowl and cover it with a clean damp cloth. Leave the dough to rest for half an hour.
4. Knead the dough again and divide it into 8 small balls. Now take the small ball into the palm of your hand and roll it into a round patty. Flour the surface of the rolling board and roll out the patty until you have 4 inch round in diameter.
5. Take a little margarine and spread it out on the top of the round. Fold it in half and then fold again into a quarter, then shape it into a round ball. Complete the same process with the remaining 7 balls.
6. Dust the rolling board with flour and place one ball on the board and sprinkle with a little flour, then roll it out to a round circle of about 7-inch in diameter.
7. Heat a cast-iron griddle or frying pan over a medium-low flame. When hot, place the chapatti on to its heated surface. Cook for about 1½ - 2 minutes, then turn it over and spread a little margarine with the back of the spoon on top of the chapatti.
8. Turn the chapatti over and cook the second side for about 2 minutes, then apply a little margarine on the second side. Turn it again briefly and cook for 45 seconds.
9. Take the chapatti off the heat and place it on the serving plate. Make all the chapattis this way and wrap them in aluminium foil to keep them warm until they are ready to be served.

Mango, Lime and passion fruit ice cream

Ingredients

3 good size ripe mangoes
4 passion fruits
1 tbsp lime juice
100ml milk
75g caster sugar
300ml whipping cream

Method

1. Peel the mangoes and cut the flesh roughly and liquidise it. It should produce 600g pulp. Sieve the mango pulp.
2. Scrape the passion fruit into the sieve and press to extract juice.
3. Add the lime juice and stir thoroughly. Chilli it.
4. Whisk the milk and sugar until the sugar dissolves. Whip the cream, then stir in the sugar mixture thoroughly.
5. Pour the mixture into the bowl of the ice-cream maker.
6. Churn for about 20 minutes until semi-frozen, add the chilled mango and keep churning until firm. Transfer to tubs and cover with the lids and freeze. It will produce two tubs of 500g.

Lemon Bread Pudding

Ingredients

6 large slices of white bread, crusts removed
and very generously buttered
1 tbsp butter
2 tbsp flaked blanched almonds
2 oz chopped mixed peel
¼ tsp ground mixed spice or allspice
rind of 2 lemons finely grated
2 tbsp soft brown sugar

Custard:

2 eggs
¼ tsp vanilla essence
few drops of almond essence
15 fl oz milk
1 tbsp sugar

Method

1. Lightly grease a medium-sized shallow baking dish.
2. Cut the bread slices into quarters. Place a third of the bread quarters, buttered sides up, in the bottom of the prepared dish. Sprinkle over the bread half the flaked almonds, peel, mixed spice, grated lemon rind and brown sugar.
3. Cover with a second layer of bread quarters. Sprinkle over the remaining almonds, peel, mixed spice, lemon rind and sugar. Cover with the remaining bread quarters, buttered sides up.
4. Preheat the oven to fairly hot temperature at Gas Mark 5 /190C/ 375F.
5. Meanwhile, make the custard. Beat the eggs, vanilla and almond essence in a medium-sized mixing bowl. Set the mixture aside.
6. Heat in a medium saucepan the milk and sugar over moderate heat. Stir well. When the sugar is dissolved and the milk is hot, remove the pan from the heat.
7. Beat the egg mixture constantly and gradually pour the hot milk into the beaten egg mixture.
8. Pour the custard through a fine wire strainer on to the bread layers in the baking dish. Set aside for fifteen minutes, or until the bread has absorbed most of the liquid.
9. Place the dish in the centre of the oven and bake the pudding for 35 to 40 minutes, or until the top is golden and crisp.
10. Remove the pudding from the oven and serve immediately, straight from the dish.

Kulfi – Indian Ice cream

Ingredients

400ml/14fl oz cans of evaporated milk
1 egg white , well whisked so that you see peaks formed
116g/4oz icing sugar
1/3 tps cardamom powder
½ tsp rose water
38g/2oz pistachios, chopped
23g/1oz flaked almonds
1 tbsp glace cherries, halved

Method

1. Place the evaporated milk can in a pan with a light lid. Fill the pan with enough water to cover three-quarters of the can. Bring it to the boil.
2. Cover and simmer for 20 minutes. Cool the can, remove and chill it in the fridge for 24 hours
3. Empty the milk into a large, chilled freezer- proof bowl. Whisk until it doubles in quantity, then fold the whisked egg white and icing sugar.
4. Gently fold in the remaining ingredients, seal the bowl with clear film and freeze for one hour.
5. Remove the ice cream from the freezer and mix well with a fork. Transfer to a serving container and freeze again. Remove from the freezer 10 minutes before serving.

Tiramasu

This Italian dessert is well-loved by my family and can be prepared with different kind of alcohol ranging from rum, coffee liqueur or brandy.

Ingredients

500g mascarpone
200ml whipping or double cream
5 tbsp of caster sugar
4 eggs yolks
200g sponge finger biscuits
4 tbsp coffee liqueur
Cocoa powder, sifted

Method

1. Soak the sponge biscuits in the coffee liqueur. Whip the cream with a tablespoonful of sugar.
2. Meanwhile, beat the egg yolks with the remaining sugar until they become creamy, then add the mascarpone little by little. Finally, add the whipped cream.
3. Arrange the soaked sponge biscuits in the base of a dessert bowl, then cover the biscuits with a layer of mascarpone cream. Place another layer of sponge biscuits and then cover with the remaining cream.
4. Sprinkle the dessert with cocoa powder and place it in the fridge for at least one hour.

Baked Pears with Cardamom

Ingredients

3 large pears, peeled, halved and cored
2 tbsp soft brown sugar
4 fl oz orange flavoured liqueur
2 tsp ground cardamom
8 oz double cream stiffly whipped

Method

1. Cut the pears into slices. Arrange them in a shallow ovenproof dish and sprinkle over the sugar.
2. Pour the liqueur over the top then sprinkle over the cardamom.
3. Preheat the oven to moderate heat at Gas Mark 4/180C/ 350F.
4. Place the dish in the oven and bake for 40 minutes, or until the pear slices are tender.
5. Transfer the pear mixture to individual serving dishes and set aside to cool completely. When the pears are cold, spoon equal amounts of the cream into each dish and serve at once.

Mango and Apricot Cheesecake

Ingredients

6 oz /170g digestive biscuits
2oz /57g melted butter
3 oz/90g dried mango slices
5 oz/150g dried apricots
8 fl oz/200ml orange juice
8fl oz / 200ml fromage frais
2 tbsp caster sugar
2 eggs

Method

1. Crush the digestive biscuits into smooth crumbs and reserve a tablespoon of biscuits for later use.
2. Mix the rest of the biscuit crumbs with the melted butter. Press into the base of a 6 inch/15 cm loose-bottomed flan case and chill it for 30 minutes.
3. Put the apricots and four ounces of orange juice in a small saucepan and bring it to the boil. Cover and simmer for five minutes. Cool the mixture for 15 minutes.
4. In a separate sauce pan put the mango slices and 4 ounces of orange juice and bring it to the boil.
5. Puree the apricots and mango slices with their liquid separately and spread two-thirds of apricot in the prepared tin as a first layer. Then spread two thirds of mango puree over it.
6. Pre-heat the oven to Gas Mark 5 190C/375F.
7. Mix the remaining fruit puree with the fromage frais, sugar and eggs. Pour the mixture over the apricots.
8. Bake the cheesecake for about one hour and ten minutes. Cool it for 10 minutes before removing from the tin and sprinkle with the reserve crumbs. Serve hot or cold. Alternatively, you can decorate the cheesecake with fresh strawberries.

Trifle

Ingredients

6 small stale slices of sponge cake
2 fl oz orange flavoured liqueur
2 tbsp fresh orange juice
10 oz sugar
10 fl oz custard
14 oz mixed fruit salad tin
5 fl oz double cream stiffly whipped

Method

1. Place the sponge slices in one layer in a large dish. Sprinkle over the liqueur and orange juice and set aside for 30 minutes, or until all the liquid has been absorbed.
2. In a heavy pan, dissolve the sugar over a low heat, shaking the pan occasionally. Increase the heat to moderate and boil the syrup, shaking the pan occasionally, until it turns to a rich golden brown.
3. Remove the pan from the heat. Place it in a bowl of hot water to keep the caramel hot.
4. Arrange one-third of the soaked sponge slices in a medium-sized serving dish. Spoon over one-third of the custard, smoothing it over evenly with the back of a spoon.
5. Lay one-third of the fruit salad over the custard to cover it completely.
6. Trickle one-third of the caramel over in a thin stream.
7. Continue making layers in the same way, ending with a layer of caramel and fruit salad.
8. Place the trifle in the refrigerator and chill it for 2 hours.
9. Fill a small forcing bag, fitted with a star-shaped nozzle, with the cream.
10. Remove the trifle from the refrigerator and pipe the cream over the top in decorative swirls. Serve immediately.

Pineapple Upside –down cake

This is an American cake in which the fruit is arranged decoratively at the bottom of the cake and the batter is poured over the top. When the cake is baked it is turned out, upside-down, to display the fruit. Serve it with whipped cream or thick cold custard.

Ingredients

5 oz butter, softened
2 tbsp soft brown sugar
1 medium-sized fresh pineapple, peeled, cored and cut into 9 rings
or 14 oz canned pineapple rings drained
9 glace- cherries
4 oz sugar
2 eggs
6 oz self-raising flour sifted
3 tbsp milk

Method

1. Lightly grease the sides of a rectangular (6 x 10 inches) cake tin, with butter.
2. Cut two tablespoons of the butter into small pieces and dot them over the base of the tin.
3. Sprinkle the brown sugar carefully over the top. Arrange the pineapple slices decoratively on top of the sugar, and place a glace cherry in the centre of each ring. Set the tin aside.
4. In a medium-sized bowl, beat the remaining butter until it is soft and creamy.
5. Add the sugar and cream to it and beat again until the mixture is light and fluffy.
6. Add the eggs, one at a time, beating well until they are thoroughly blended. Using a large spoon, fold in the flour. Stir in enough of the milk to give the batter a dropping consistency.
7. Preheat the oven to a moderate temperature at Gas Mark 4/180C /350 F.
8. Carefully spoon the batter into the cake tin, so that the cherries are not dislodged. Smooth the top of the batter with a flat-bladed knife.
9. Place the cake tin in the centre of the oven and bake the cake for 50-60 minutes or until the cake is golden brown. Check the cake by inserting a skewer into the centre of the cake. If the skewer comes out clean then the cake is ready.
10. Remove the tin from the oven and allow the cake to cool for 5 minutes. Run a knife around the sides of the cake. Invert a serving dish over the cake tin and reverse the two. The cake should slide out easily. Decorate each cherry with two angelica leaves, if desired.

Summer Pudding

Ingredients

2 lbs raspberries, cleaned
1 tsp butter
10 fl oz /1½ cup double cream
4 oz caster sugar
4 fl oz milk
8 slices of white bread, crusts removed

Method

1. Grease a deep pudding basin.
2. Place the raspberries in a large mixing bowl and sprinkle them with the sugar. Set aside.
3. Sprinkle a little of the milk over each slice of the bread to moisten it.
4. Line the basin with two-thirds of the bread slices, overlapping the edges slightly. Pour the raspberries into the basin and arrange the remaining bread slices on top to cover the raspberries.
5. Place a sheet of greaseproof paper on top of the basin and put a plate and some weight on top. Put the pudding in the refrigerator to chill for at least 8 hours or overnight.
6. Remove the pudding from the refrigerator and lift off the weight and the plate. Remove and discard the greaseproof paper. Invert a serving plate over the top of the basin and, holding the two firmly together; reverse them giving a sharp shake. The pudding should slide out easily.
7. In a separate serving bowl, beat the cream with a wire whisk until it is thick, but not stiff. Serve the pudding immediately with cream.

This dessert is light and refreshing, especially during summer period.

Ingredients

4 fresh peaches, blanched, peeled,
halved and stoned
3 tbsp double cream
1 tbsp caster sugar
¼ tsp vanilla essence
1 oz dark dessert chocolate, finely grated
4 tbsp blanched slivered almonds

Method

1. In individual dessert dishes, arrange two peach halves with rounded sides down. Set aside.

2. In a mixing bowl, whisk the cream, sugar and vanilla essence together with a wire whisk or rotary beater until the mixture forms soft peaks.

3. With a spoon, or spatula gently fold half of the chocolate and half of the almonds into the cream mixture.

4. Place a little of the mixture in each peach half.

5. Sprinkle each dish with equal amounts of the remaining grated chocolate and almonds.

6. Chill in the refrigerator for at least 1 hour before serving.

Poached Plums in Cider

This is a delicious dessert for warm summer days. It can be served with extra sugar or honey and plenty of cream.

Ingredients

1 kg /2lb1.4 oz plums,
halved and stoned
1 litre / 1 ¾ pt dry cider
1 inch cinnamon stick
175g /6oz caster sugar

Method

1. Preheat the oven Gas Mark 2 /150C/300F.

2. Arrange the halved plums in a snug, single layer in a roasting tin.

3. Put the cider, cinnamon stick and sugar into a saucepan and stir over a moderate heat until the sugar has dissolved.

4. Bring to the boil and simmer for 10 minutes to make light syrup.

5. Pour over the plums and place in the oven while still hot.

6. Baste once or twice as they cook, until very tender.

7. Bake for 20-25 minutes, depending on the ripeness of the plums.

8. Lift the plums out with a slotted spoon and pile into a shallow serving dish.

9. Put the roasting tin on the hob and boil the juices hard until reduced by about half.

10. Pour the juices over the plums and leave to cool. Serve with cream.

Pineapple and mango crumble

Ingredients

12 oz/25g ripe mango
8 oz/350g fresh peeled pineapple
1 oz /25g unsalted butter
2 oz / 55g caster sugar

For the crumble topping

8 oz/225g plain flour
4oz/115g brown or demerrara sugar
4 oz/115g unsalted diced butter

Method

1. Carefully peel off the skin of the mango and cut into slices then dice each slice into 1 cm or ½ in pieces.

2. Cut the top-notch of the pineapple and strip off the skin by cutting thin strips from the top to the bottom of the fruit, making sure that the eyes are cut off. Cut the pineapple in half lengthways then cut each half to the same size of the mango and mix the fruit. Butter a pie dish generously and place the fruit into the pie dish and pat down.

3. Sprinkle the caster sugar over to form a flat bed (the amount of sugar you need depends on the taste of the individual and the sweetness of the fruit.

4. Make the crumble topping by rubbing the cold butter dice into the flour to form a breadcrumb-like mixture. Stir in the brown sugar. Sprinkle some of the crumble topping over the fruit. Pat down firmly and then sprinkle the rest on top.

5. Preheat the oven to Gas Mark 4/180C/350F. Bake in the preheated oven for 15 minutes. Reduce the temperature of the oven to Gas Mark 3/160C/325F and bake for about a further 25 to 30 minutes. Serve with custard or ice cream.

Pears in white wine with chocolate sauce

Ingredients

8 pears
1 bottle white wine
165g/ 5 oz sugar
Peel of one lemon

For chocolate sauce

300g dark bitter chocolate
1 small glass Marsala wine
1 ½ tbsp butter

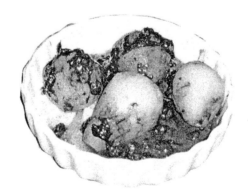

Method

1. Peel the pears and cut them in halves. Place them in a sauce pan and pour the white wine and add the lemon peel. Boil them vigorously for 15 minutes.

2. Now add the sugar and stir gently then boil for a further five minutes.

3. Remove the saucepan from the heat and allow the pears and the wine mixture to cool before putting them into the fridge to chill thoroughly.

4. To prepare the sauce, place the bowl on top of the saucepan of boiling water and melt the chocolate together with the butter then stir in the Marsala wine.

5. Take the pears from the fridge and drain them from the juice and pour the hot chocolate sauce over and serve. You can preserve these pears for a few days in the refrigerator and use them within a week.

Caramel Sauce

Ingredients

6 tbs granulated or caster sugar
6 tbs water

Method

1. Put the sugar and water into a heavy saucepan. Stir over on a low heat until the sugar has dissolved.
2. If the sugar and water splash against the sides of the saucepan brush with a pastry brush dipped in cold water.
3. Allow the sugar and water syrup to boil steadily until golden brown.
4. Pour the mixture in the individual deep dishes to make Crème Brûlée.

Crème Brûlée

Ingredients

10 fl oz/300ml milk
4 eggs
1 tbsp sugar
10 fl oz /300ml thick cream

For the topping:

2 tbsp blanched almonds
2 tbsp sieved icing sugar

Method

1. Make caramel sauce as shown on page 222. Leave in the saucepan to cool slightly. Add the milk, heat gently until blended with the caramel.
2. Beat the eggs with the sugar and cream, add caramel and milk.
3. Strain the mixture into a deep ovenproof or soufflé dish.
4. Bake for 1½ to 2 hours at Gas Mark 3 /325F/170C or until firm.
5. Top with almonds and sugar and brown for a few minutes under the grill.

ENGLISH TEACAKES

These are simple easy recipes for teacakes. My daughter prepares some of these teacakes for her two young boys. I thought it would be an idea to have these in my book.

Simple Sponge cake

Ingredients

175g /7 oz caster sugar
3 large eggs
50g/2oz butter
3tbs water
½ tsp vanilla essence
125g/5oz plain flour

For the topping

3tbs jam
Icing sugar sieved

Method

1. Grease two (18cm/ 7in) sandwich tins and line the bases with greaseproof paper.
2. Whisk the sugar and eggs together with an electric whisk for 10 minutes.
3. Put the butter and water into a small pan and heat gently until the butter has melted.
4. Pour into the whisked mixture with vanilla essence and whisk for half a minute.
5. Sieve in the flour and fold into the mixture.
6. Turn into the prepared tins and give each tin a sharp tap to settle the mixture.
7. Pre-heat the oven and bake in a moderate hot heat for 20-25 minutes at Gas mark 5 , 190C/375F or until well risen and the cakes spring back when lightly pressed.
8. Leave the cakes in the tins for 2-3 minutes, then turn out on to a wire rack to cool.
9. When cold sandwich together with jam and sprinkle with icing sugar.

Orange or Lemon Cake

Ingredients

130g / 4 oz margarine or butter
130g / 4 oz sugar
130g / 4 oz self-raising flour
2 eggs

For the topping:

2 tbsp sugar
Juice of an orange or lemon .

Method

2. Cream the butter and sugar together.
3. Slowly add the beaten eggs, beating well.
4. Fold in the flour.
5. Bake in a 1 lb loaf tin for 30-40 minutes at Gas Mark 3, 170C/ 325F.
6. Warm and mix together 2 tablespoons of sugar and orange or lemon juice. When the cake is cooked and still hot, prick the top all over and pour on the syrup. (Use extra sugar or juice to taste)

For lemon cake, use lemon juice instead of orange juice.

This is a nice and moist loaf that can be buttered to enhance its taste. It keeps well for a week if kept in a sealed biscuit tin.

Ingredients

120g / large cup self-raising flour
8 fl oz / large cup skimmed milk
80g / large cup coconut
60g / ½ cup sugar (less, if preferred)
100g chopped apricots
100g mixed fruit

Method

1. Grease a 2lb loaf tin, line with grease-proof paper, well greased

2. Combine all the ingredients. Place in the tin.

3. Cook at Gas Mark 4/ 180 C/ 350F for one hour.

Rich Fruit Cake

Ingredients

250g / 9 oz plain flour
½ teaspoon salt
1 tsp ground mixed spice
300g / 9 oz butter
265g / 8 oz dark brown sugar
2 tbsp black treacle
½ tsp vanilla essence
4 large eggs, lightly beaten
2 lb mixed dried fruit
112g / 4 oz chopped mixed peel
168g / 6 oz cherries halved
112g / 4 oz blanched almonds, chopped
3 tablespoon brandy

Method

1. Grease an 8 inch round tin and line the base and sides with a double layer of greaseproof paper. A band of brown paper tied round the outside of the tin will prevent the cake from becoming too browned while cooking.

2. Sieve together the flour, salt and mixed spice. Cream the butter, sugar, treacle and vanilla essence together until light and fluffy.

3. Beat in the eggs, a little at a time, adding a teaspoon of the flour with the last amount.

4. Fold in the remaining flour, then all the fruit and almonds. Turn the mixture into the prepared cake tin and make it slightly hollow in the centre.

5. Bake in a cool oven at Gas Mark 2 150C/ 300F for about 3-4 hours.

6. Test after 3 hours by inserting a skewer into the centre. If the skewer comes out clean the cake is cooked. Remove from the oven on to a wire rack and leave to cool. Make a few holes in the top of the cake with a skewer and pour over the brandy. Wrap the cake in greaseproof paper and store in an airtight tin for at least a week before using.

Ingredients

200g / 6 oz margarine (preferably soft)
160g / 5 oz self-raising flour
200g / 6 oz caster sugar
160g / 6 oz drinking chocolate powder
3 large eggs
3 tbsp boiling water

Method

1. Place all the ingredients in a mixing bowl then add the boiling water.

2. Stir slowly at first then beat well.   (if using electric mixer, beat at the maximum speed for 2 minutes.)

3. Grease an 8-inch deep cake tin and line it with greased paper.

4. Put the mixture into the prepared cake tin.

5. Bake in a pre-heated oven at Gas Mark 4/ 180C/ 350F for 1¼ - 1½ hours, until firm.

6. Cool a little before turning out of the tin.

7. The cake can be decorated with icing sugar, if desired.

Easter Cake

Easter cake is as much a part of the Easter festival. It is customary to make an Easter Cake to celebrate Easter Day and the end of the Lenten Fast.

Ingredients

8 oz / 225 gm self-raising flour
4 oz /115 gm plain flour
4 standard eggs
1 tsp ground mixed spice
8oz /225gm sultanas
8 oz /225 gm raisins
8 oz/ 225 gm currants
2 oz/ 50 gm chopped peel

4 oz/ 115 gm ground almonds
4 oz/ 115 gm glace cherries, halved
8 oz/ 225 gm butter
8 oz /225 gm light soft brown sugar
juice of one orange
1 ½ lb / 675gm almond paste
2 tbsp of apricot jam, warmed and sieved

Method

1. Grease and line with grease paper a 10 inch /25 cm round deep cake tin.

2. Sift plain and self-raising flour with the mixed spice.

3. Mix the sultanas, raisins, currants, peel and cherries in a bowl. Sprinkle two spoonfuls of the flour mixture over the fruit and add the ground almonds and mix well.

4. Cream together the butter and sugar until very soft and pale. Carefully beat in the eggs, one at a time, adding a little of the flour mixture after each addition to prevent the mixture from curdling. Fold in the remaining flour using a large metal spoon. Then fold the remaining mixture and the orange juice.

5. Turn the mixture into the tin and spread it evenly with a palette knife.

6. Pre-heat the oven to Gas Mark 3/ 160C/ 325F.

7. Bake the cake for approximately 3½ to 3 ¾ hours. Cover the top of the cake loosely with a piece of foil after the first two hours to prevent it from browning.

8. To check if the cake is ready, insert a metal skewer into the middle of the cake. If the cake is cooked, the skewer will come out clean without any sticky mixture clinging to it.

9. Remove the cake from the tin and cool it on a wire rack.

10. Brush the top of the cake with a thin layer of apricot jam. Roll out a third of the almond paste to cover the top, and place on top of the jam. Use the remaining almond paste to decorate the top of the cake.

Rich Chocolate cake

Ingredients

4 oz butter

6 oz dark cooking chocolate, broken into pieces

6 oz sugar

3 oz flour

1 tsp vanilla essence

6 egg yolks

8 egg whites, stiffly whipped

6 tbsp apricot jam

Chocolate Icing

8 oz dark cooking chocolate, broken into pieces

4 fl oz double cream

12 oz icing sugar

Method

1. Melt the chocolate pieces in a heatproof bowl set over a pan of simmering water. Remove the pan from the heat and lift the bowl out of the pan and set aside.

2. In a mixing bowl, beat the butter and the sugar together until they are light and fluffy. Beat in the melted chocolate and the vanilla essence.

3. Gradually beat in the egg yolks, one at a time, adding a tablespoon of flour with each yolk.

4. Fold in the remaining flour, and then the egg whites. Mix well.

5. Grease a 9 inch cake tin with a removable base. Spoon the batter into the prepared cake tin and smooth over the top with the back of the spoon.

6. Preheat the oven to Gas Mark 4/180C/350F. Place the tin in the centre of the oven and bake for 50 to 55 minutes or until a skewer inserted into the centre of the cake comes out clean.

7. Remove the cake from the oven and set it aside to cool in the tin for half an hour.

8. Turn the cake out of the tin on to a wire rack and slice it in half, crosswise. Set aside to cool completely.

9. In the meantime, place a small saucepan over low heat and melt the apricot jam, stirring constantly. Remove from the heat and set aside to cool to lukewarm

10. Now make the chocolate icing. In a heatproof bowl set over a pan of simmering water, melt the chocolate pieces over low heat. Remove the pan from the heat and lift the bowl out of the pan. Set aside to cool for 10 to 12 minutes. Beat in the cream and icing sugar, beating until the mixture is smooth.

11. Using a flat-bladed knife, spread half the apricot glaze over the top of the bottom cake half and sandwich the two halves together. Spread the rest of the glaze over the top and sides of the cake.

12. Wash and wipe the knife. Spread the chocolate icing over the top and sides of the cake, ensuring the icing is smooth. Place the cake on a serving dish and set aside to cool for about 2 hours or until the icing has set.

With the same recipe you can make fruit and cheese scones. For fruit scones: add 2 oz of sultanas or currants and 1 oz of sugar after rubbing in the fat. For cheese scones: sieve dry mustard powder with the flour and add 3oz finely grated Cheddar cheese after rubbing in the fat.

Ingredients

225g / 8 oz plain flour
½ tsp salt
1 tsp bicarbonate of soda
2 tsp cream of tartar
1½ oz margarine
¼ pint milk

Method

1. Sieve the flour, salt, bicarbonate of soda and cream of tartar into a bowl. Rub in the margarine until the mixture resembles fine breadcrumbs.

2. Add enough milk to form into soft but not sticky dough, using a round-bladed knife to mix.

3. Turn on to a floured surface and knead very lightly.

4. Roll out the dough ½ inch thick. Cut out into rounds 2 inch in diameter using a pastry cutter.

5. Place on lightly-floured baking sheets and sprinkle with a little extra flour.

6. Bake in a pre-heated oven at Gas Mark 7 / 220C / 425F for about 12 minutes or until risen and golden in colour.

7. Serve warm or cold with butter and jam or cream and jam.

Banana Tea Bread

Ingredients

225g / 8 oz self-raising flour, sieved
½ tsp mixed spice
130g / 4 oz margarine
130g / 4 oz brown sugar
2 large eggs
1 lb bananas, mashed

Method

1. Beat together the margarine and sugar.

2. Beat in one egg then add the second egg with a little flour. Beat well.

3. Beat in the mashed bananas and mixed spice. Fold in rest of the flour.

4. Put the mixture in 2lb loaf tin.

5. Bake at Gas Mark 4 180C / 350 F for 1 - 1 ½ hour.

Coconut and Cherry Cake

Ingredients

12 oz /300g self-raising flour
Pinch of salt
6 oz /150g margarine
8 oz glace cherries quartered
2 oz / 50g desiccated coconut
6 oz / 150g caster sugar
2 large eggs, lightly beaten
¼ pint / 125 ml milk

Method

1. Grease an 8 inch (20 cm) cake tin and line the base with greased-proof paper.

2. Sieve together the flour and salt. Rub in the margarine until the mixture resembles fine breadcrumbs.

3. Toss the cherries in the coconut and add to the mixture with the sugar. Mix lightly

4. Add the eggs to the mixture with most of the milk. Beat well, then add some more milk to give a soft dropping consistency.

5. Turn into the prepared tin, level off and bake in a pre-heated oven Gas mark 4 180C/ 350 F for 1½ hours or until well risen and golden brown.

6. Leave in the tin for 5 minutes, then turn out on to a wire rack to cool.

Victoria Sandwich

Ingredients

110g / 4 oz self-raising flour
110g / 4 oz butter or margarine
100g / 4 oz caster sugar
2 large eggs beaten lightly
¼ teaspoon vanilla essence

Method

1. Grease two 6 inch sandwich tins and line the bases with greaseproof paper.

2. Sieve the flour. Cream the butter and sugar together in a bowl, either by hand with a wooden spoon or with an electric beater, until the mixture is very light and fluffy.

3. Gradually beat in the eggs, blended with the vanilla essence, adding a spoonful of the sieved flour with the last amount. Carefully fold in the sieved flour.

4. Divide the mixture between the two sandwich tins and bake in a pre-heated oven (Gas Mark 4 180C / 350F) for 20-25 minutes or until the cakes are golden brown in colour.

5. Remove from the oven and leave to cool for a couple of minutes, then turn out on to a wire rack and leave until quite cold.

6. Sandwich the cakes together with jam or cream and sprinkle the top with a little sugar.

Butterfly Cakes

Ingredients

100g /4 oz self-raising flour
100g /4 oz caster sugar
100g / 4 oz butter or margarine
a pinch of salt
2 standard eggs, lightly beaten

For the filling:

100g / 4 oz icing sugar, sieved
50g /2 oz butter
Vanilla essence

Method

1. Sieve the flour and salt. Cream the butter or margarine and sugar until light and fluffy.
2. Gradually beat in the eggs one by one, adding a tablespoon of the flour with the last amount. Fold in the remaining flour.
3. Place 15 – 16 paper cases on a baking sheet.
4. Divide the mixture between the cake cases and bake in a pre-heated (moderately hot) oven (Gas Mark 5, 190C/ 375F) for 15-20 minutes or until well risen and golden brown. Allow the cases to cool.
5. When the cakes are quite cold, cut out a circle from the top of each cake, using a sharp knife. Then cut each of these circles in half.
6. Cream the butter and beat in the icing sugar and a few drops of vanilla essence.
7. Spoon a little butter cream into the centre of each cake and press two semi-circular pieces into it to look like butterfly wings.

Apricot Cheesecake

Ingredients

4 oz /125g digestive biscuits
1½ oz /40g butter melted
5 oz / 150g dried apricots
4 fl oz orange juice
7 oz fromage frais
1 tbsp caster sugar
2 eggs

Method

1. Crush the digestive biscuits into smooth crumbs and reserve a tablespoon of biscuits crumbs for later use.
2. Mix the rest of the biscuits crumbs with the melted butter. Press into the base of a 6 inch / 15 cm loose-bottomed flan case and chill it for 30 minutes.
3. Put the apricots and orange juice in a small saucepan and bring it to the boil. Cover and simmer for 5 minutes. Cool for 15 minutes.
4. Puree the apricots with their liquid and spread two-thirds in the prepared tin.
5. Pre-heat the oven to Gas Mark 5 190C /375 F.
6. Mix the remaining puree with the fromage frais, sugar and eggs. Pour the mixture over the apricots.
7. Bake the cheesecake for about 35-40 minutes. Cool for 5 minutes before removing from the tin and sprinkle with the reserve crumbs. Serve hot or cold. Alternatively, you can decorate the cheese cake with fresh raspberry or strawberry.

Ingredients

4 oz/100g cashew nuts chopped
2 oz/50g oz whole hazelnuts
3 large eggs, lightly beaten
5 oz/ 125g self-raising flour
2 oz/ 50g caster sugar
2 oz/ 50 g butter softened
4 oz/ 100g clear honey

Method

1. Scatter the nuts on a baking tray and put into a moderately hot oven for 10 minutes. Allow to cool then rub the nuts between your hands to remove the brown skin. Chop finely. Alternatively, you can buy the chopped hazelnuts.

2. Pre-heat the oven at Gas Mark 4, 180 C / 350 F.

3. Well grease and line the base of a shallow cake tin 8 inches (20 cm) in diameter.

4. Blend the flour, sugar and eggs together in a bowl. Stir in the nuts, then the butter and honey. Turn the mixture into the prepared tin and bake in a moderate hot oven for 40-45 minutes, or until golden brown.

5. Leave the cake in the tin for 5 minutes, then turn out and cool on a wire rack.

Orange Madeira Cake with Caraway Seeds

Ingredients

14 oz/ 400 g plain flour
2 oz /57g rice flour
4 large eggs lightly beaten
Pinch of salt
1 tbs orange rind finely grated
1 tbs baking powder
1oz /284g butter or margarine
1oz / 284g sugar
1 tbs caraway seeds
6 fl oz orange juice

Method

1. Pre-heat the oven to Gas Mark 4 180CC/160F

2. Grease a 6 in (15 cm) cake tin and line the base with greaseproof paper.

3. Cream the butter, sugar and orange rind until light and fluffy. Beat in each egg at a time. Fold in the flour, then orange juice to give a soft dropping consistency.

4. Turn the mixture into the prepared tin. Bake in a moderate oven for 45 minutes, then open the oven door to sprinkle caraway seeds on top of the cake. Bake for further one hour until well risen and golden brown.

5. Leave in the tin for five minutes, then turn out on to a wire rack to cool.

6. Madeira cake can be cooked with different variations; such as omit orange rind and replace with lemon rind and caraway seeds, or omit the orange rind and caraway seeds, add 1 teaspoon of almond essence and sprinkle with flaked almonds before baking.

Ingredients

8 oz /200 g butter
8 oz /200g caster sugar
4 large eggs lightly beaten
8 oz /200g self-raising flour

For the coffee syrup:

4 oz / 100g sugar
½ pint water
3 tbsp strong coffee
4 tbsp rum

To decorate:

½ pint double cream lightly whipped
walnuts halves

Method

1. Well grease an 8 inch (20 cm) cake tin then line the base with greaseproof paper.

2. Cream the butter and sugar until light and fluffy. Gradually beat in the eggs, adding a tablespoon of the flour with the last amount. Sieve in the flour then fold in carefully.

3. Turn the mixture into the prepared tin and level off.

4. Pre-heat the oven at Gas Mark 5 / 190C / 375F.

5. Bake in a pre-heated oven for 50-55 minutes or until the cake is golden brown and springs back when lightly pressed. Allow to cool in the tin for five minutes.

6. While the cake is cooking dissolve the sugar and water in the pan. Then add the coffee and place the pan over a low heat and bring it to the boil then add the rum. Take the pan off the heat and keep the mixture warm.

7. Turn the cake out of the tin on to a serving plate. Pierce it all over with a skewer then pour over some of the warm coffee syrup. Leave this to soak in, then pour over some more and continue to do this until the cake has absorbed all the syrup. Leave the cake to stand for at least 6 hours.

8. Spread the whipped cream all over the top and sides of the cake and decorate the top with walnut halves.

FOOD GLOSSARY

ENGLISH	KONKANI
Almonds	Amena
Aniseed	Saunf
Aperitif	Ruch
Apple	Apple
Apricot	Apricot
Asafoetida	Hing
Aubergine	Vaanghem
Baked	Bazlolo
Baked potatoes	Bazlole botate
Baker	Poder
Baking powder	Caratin
Balls of minced meat	Kofta
Banana	Keli
Bay leaf	Tej patta
Beef	Gaiechem maas
Beer	Cervej
Biscuit	Biscuit
Bitter gourd	Karela
Black-eyed beans	Iril
Boil	Ukdunk
Bombay duck	Bombil
Bottle	Bathli
Bowl	Supero
Brain	Mende
Brandy	Brandy
Bread	Undo/ pao
Breakfast	Nasto
Bream	Paloo
Butter	Mosko
Butter beans stew	Feijoada
Cabbage	Repolho
Cake	Bol

ENGLISH	KONKANI
Capsicum	Mote misango
Caraway seeds	Shahjeera
Cardamom	Elchi
Carrot	Gajar
Cashewnut	Caju bio
Catfish	Sangtam
Cauliflour	Full-gobi
Cheese	Queijo
Chef	Cozinheiro
Cherries	Cherries
Chicken	Combi
Chicken soup	Combicho sopa
Chilly	Mirchi
Chocolate	Chocolete
Chops	Chops
Cinnamon	Tikki
Clams	Tisro
Clarified butter	Ghee
Cloves	Kalafuram
Cluster beans	Gavar
Coconut	Nal
Coconut cake	Batica
Coconut sugar	Gord
Coffee	Café
Cold	Tond
Conjee	Pez
Coriander	Cutmiri
Crabs	Kooli
Cucumber	Teuxem
Cumin	Jeera
Cup	Chicre
Curd	Dhaim
Curry leaves	Curry patta
Dried and powdered shrimps	Kishmar

ENGLISH	KONKANI
Drink	Piunk
Drumstick	Xengo
Dry coconut	Kopra
Eels	Bare
Eggs	Tantia
Fat	Gordur
Fenugreek	Methi
Fiery sauce for meat with roasted spices	Xacuti
Fish	Nishtem
Fish curry	Nishtaychi corri
Flat bread	Bakhri
Flour	Peet
Food	Jevon
Fork	Garaf
Fowl/chicken	Combi
Fried bread	Poori
Fried eels	Toulele bare
Fried fish	Bazloleo nishtem
Fried squids	Bazeloleo mankio
Fruit	Frut/follam
Fruit juice	Follam ros
Frying pan	Tava
Garlic	Loson
Gherkin	Bimbli
Ginger	Alem
Glass	Glass
Goa sausages	Chourisso
Goan Christmas cake	Bebinca
Goat	Bokdi
Good	Borem
Gram	Chana
Green peas	Mattar
Green plantains	Kachcha kela

ENGLISH	KONKANI
Green-chilliy	Misango
Grocer	Bajiwalla
Groundnuts	Moong phalli
Guava	Per
Ham	Presunta
Hot chocolate	Gorom chocolate
Jackfruit	Ponos
Jaggery	Gord
Jam	Jam
Knife	Piscathi
Kingfish	Eison
Lady finger	Bendhi
Lemon	Limbu
Lemon fish	Modso
Lemon rind	Limbu ka chilka
Lentils	Dal
Lettuce	Salad bhaji
Lime	Limboo
Lobster	Ching-go
Lunch	Don paranchem jeuvon
Macaroni	Macroni
Mackerel	Bangdo
Mango	Ambó
Mango powder	Amchoor
Meal	Jevon
Meat croquettes	Massache croket
Milk	Dhud
Mince lamb or beef	Keema
Mint leaf	Pudina
Mint tea	Peppermint chai
Mullet	Shevto
Mussels	Xinnanio/ zob
Mustard	Rai
Nutmeg	Zaifal

ENGLISH	KONKANI
Oil	Tel
Olive oil	Axeitachem tel
Onion	Kando/piao
Oyster	Calvan
Pancakes stuffed with fresh coconut	Alebele
Peppercorn	Mirem
Pickled pork seasoned with hot spices	Sorpatel
Pigling	Leitao
Pineapple	Ananas
Plate	Boshi
Pomfret	Pomplit or pitorshi
Poppy seeds	Khus khus
Pork	Ducra maas
Pork marinated hot-sour curry	Vindaloo
Potasium nitrate	Saltpetre
Potato and cabbage soup	Caldo verde
Potato	Botate
Prawns	Sungtam
Prawn crusty pie	Apa de camarao
Pumpkin	Dudhi
Pungent	Tik
Radish	Molo
Raisins	Kismis
Red chilly	Lal mirchi
Red chilly sauce	Balchao
Red spinach	Tamdi bhaji
Red pumpkin	Tambdi dudhi
Restaurant	Khannavol
Rice	Tandoor/sheeth
Rice with saffron	Biriyani
Ridge gourd	Gonsaim
Roast	Assada

ENGLISH	KONKANI
Roast beef	Gaecho assad
Rock salmon	Mori
Rock fish	Gobro
Salt	Mit
Salted	Kharem
Sardine	Tarle
Sausage	Chouriso
Semolia	Sooji
Shark	Mori
Shellfish	Tisreo
Skate	Vagolem
Snaper	Tamso
English	Konkani
Spaghetti	Sphagetti
Spicy fried chicken or fish	Cafreal
Spinach	Palak
Squid	Mankio
Stuffed aubergines	Bharli vaangi
Stuffed	Recheada
Stuffing	Rechear
Suckling	Leitao
Sugar	Sacor
Sweet	God
Sweet curry braised in yoghurt	Korma
Sweet potato	Kongham
Syrup	Sarope
Table	Mez
Tamarind	Ambtan
Tartlet forms	Forminhas
Tea	Chai
Thyme	Hasha
Tiger prawns	Vodlim Sungtam
Toddy	Sur
Tomato	Tamatam

ENGLISH	KONKANI
Tongue	Jib
Tuna	Bodorn
Turmeric	Olod
Turnip	Shalgam
Unleavened bread	Chapatti or roti
Utensils	Aidon
Vanilla	Vanille
Vegetable	Torkari
Vegetable stew	Vanaspat stew
Vinegar	Inagre
Warm	Gorom
Watermelon	Kangham
White leavened bread	Naan
Whiskey	Whiskey
Wine	Vinho

RECIPE LIST

Following the success of the first publication entitled "The Goanese Fusion Flavours" in the United Kingdom; the 'Delight of Goa' covers 210 authentic dishes illustrated with colour photographs from the distinctive and varied cuisines of Asia, Africa and Europe. This second publication has been exclusively produced for the Goan people with 30 extra recipes. This cookery book would also appeal to the many Indian connoisseurs and western folk who visit the wonderful State of Goa.

Delight of Goa has wonderful recipes with essential information on ingredients and cooking techniques. The easy–to-follow instructions ensure success every time you cook. There are dishes for all occasions including starters, delicious fish, vegetable and meat main courses, selected preserves and pickles and luscious desserts from three continents.

It is my greatest joy to publish this edition in Goa as a token of love to my motherland. I was born and brought up in Goa. At the age of 22 years I left Goa to be married in Uganda, East Africa and have been living abroad with my family ever since. My family and I love Goan food and we visit Goa every year to enjoy the peace, good climate, golden beaches and the exotic foods of Goa.